A House in the Country

A
HOUSE
IN THE
COUNTRY

PETER PENNOYER
KATIE RIDDER

WITH
ANNE WALKER

PHOTOGRAPHY BY
ERIC PIASECKI

✷

THE VENDOME PRESS
NEW YORK

CONTENTS

INTRODUCTION

To tell the story of our country house, Katie and I felt that we should start by explaining how we got to the point where we were able to embark on a project that seemed, on the face of it, such a risky idea. The goal, a house of our own design where we could get away from it all, made sense, but we wondered how we would find the time and enlist the help of our colleagues when we and our offices were so busy.

The first hurdle was the prospect of a husband and wife collaborating on an aesthetic project that seemed, at best, like a concept for a reality show and, at worst, like a surefire way to doom a marriage. A common reaction, among those who don't know us very well, to the news that we designed the place together, was a look that said: "It must have been hell." And though the process was not without drama, none of it came from within our marriage. Each of us gave the other space. Katie trusted my team and me on the architecture, and I trusted her and her team on the decoration and garden. Advice was voluntary.

Another challenge was the architect's version of the doctor's rule not to operate on their own and certainly not on themselves. That commonsense dictum in medicine is equally applicable to architecture, though less so to interior design. Considering the fact that architects are generally well equipped by training and disposition to make houses, it is revealing that so few choose to do so for themselves. Though I don't like to admit it, I think architects need the discipline of a real client. The client provides a program, a budget, a schedule, and aesthetic clues or parameters. These limitations set the ground rules for the design. Freed from these constraints, I feared that the process of focusing our needs into a program, parsing a budget, and adhering to a schedule would be next to impossible.

I also wanted to avoid building a typical architect's house—the kind that seems to be designed to prove a point by eschewing comfort, by choosing the novel over the familiar. All too aware of the peril of being my own client, I managed to work around it by treating the house like any other project in my office—with Katie serving as my alter-client and my colleagues remaining front and center. In this way, my sketches and my program were regarded—as they would have been on any project—as just one ingredient in the collaboration.

Katie had more experience designing for us, but she realized that the stakes were higher in a house that was entirely of our creation. That magical exercise she calls scheming, when she lays out swatches of fabric and samples of finishes, was more challenging. She also had to contend with making my collections of everything from curiosities to nineteenth-century sculpture part of the scheme.

The woodland garden runs along the hedgerow north of the farm fields. New sugar maples, dogwood, magnolia, redbuds, and *Stewartias* were planted among the existing oaks.

Each of us found a way of meeting in the middle, often making small compromises that turned out to be the best elements of the house. These accommodations—of my sense of architecture to Katie's taste and of Katie's eye to my sense of interior decoration—would have been hard for either of us to imagine when we were starting our careers.

Katie grew up in Silicon Valley before the silicon chip. Her hometown, Saratoga, California, could barely be described as a suburb because San Jose was barely a city. Her family's white clapboard house was set next to fruit and walnut tree orchards. Across the garden and beyond the pool, a large barn sheltered Rosie the goat, Buttons the horse, and animals from the family menagerie, which included a turtle, three cats, and a golden retriever. As publisher of the *San Jose Mercury News*, Katie's father was at the center of events as the area grew from a backwater into the storied capital of computing and software. When she was in college, Katie spent her summers at the paper in the production department, at one point helping to plan for the expansion of the presses. This early exposure to the newspaper's operations gave her an important introduction to business.

Katie's interest in decorating started with a passion for fabrics, patterns, and color. She loved her family's comfortable house, but she also admired houses she saw on family trips. Her grandparents lived in a rambling Shingle Style house in St. Paul, Minnesota, decorated with antiques and Persian carpets that reflected their New York City roots. She recalls old-fashioned rooms with collections of cloisonné and enameled snuffboxes in the paneled living room and library. Her great-uncle lived nearby in a grander house decorated with European antiques, silks, and brocades—a contrast to the more relaxed style typical of the California of her childhood.

Katie was always making things. When her parents gave her a sewing machine for her thirteenth birthday, she tackled ambitious projects like elaborate quilts. For an art show, she sewed "soft sculptures"—quilted pillows in the form of fish with hinged scales. As a cottage enterprise, she offered a line of earrings she made by joining trimming tassels to earring posts. This love of making things gave her an appreciation of craft and artisanship that would inform her whole career.

One of the colorful quilted "soft sculpture" pillows that Katie sewed to sell at an art show as a teenager. This one never found a buyer.

Katie realized early on that she would be a New Yorker. In 1972, at age eleven, she accompanied her parents and grandparents on a trip to New York, fell in love with the city, and decided she would return someday and make her life there. She liked places that excited her imagination, and she disliked bland design. In high school, she painted a row of identical ranch houses emblazoned with lines from Malvina Reynolds's song "Little Boxes": "There's a green one and a pink one / And a blue one . . . / And they're all made out of ticky tacky / And they all look just the same."

Katie's interest in design and art was greatly stimulated by travels to Europe, South America, and Japan with her family. As an art history major at USC, her approach was, by her own admission, less academic and more aesthetic than that of many of her classmates. Whereas they seemed to be on a quest for esoteric knowledge and focused primarily on theory, Katie was more interested in engaging directly with the art. For her, a painting was about color, form, and composition. She was especially entranced by the work of the

Fauves; their wild brushstrokes and searing, vivid colors, as well as the naïve charm of their simple compositions, all hit a nerve. Matisse's work from this period was a revelation to her, and she also admired the work of André Derain, Georges Braque, and Raoul Dufy. Every painting she studied informed Katie about color, form, line, and pattern, enriching her sense of design.

In 1984, straight out of college, Katie moved to New York, where she landed a job at Condé Nast as an assistant to the architecture critic Martin Filler at *House & Garden*. Exposure to Filler, who was and remains one of the most respected observers of architecture in the country, provided a strong connection to the architectural side of the design world. But her real interest lay in houses and interiors. Under editor in chief Lou Gropp, *House & Garden* in the 1980s covered both the long-established decorating firms such as Parish-Hadley and younger and emerging talents like Jed Johnson.

Determined to immerse herself in the work of both the editors and the decorators, Katie would retreat to the art department, where she would pore over the files on each story to understand the raw material that was the basis of each issue.

As an assistant, she was involved in the smallest details of every story. Projects by firms known to the editors poured in the door, and new designers sent photographs over the transom. Katie scouted new stories, visiting the houses and seeing with her own eyes whether the projects were worth covering. On photo shoots, she worked with the designer and the photographer to adjust the arrangement of furniture, editing out pieces that distracted from the visual message of each shot and choosing the best camera angles.

This focus on perfecting each shot was especially painstaking in those pre-Photoshop days—once the film was exposed, the picture was final. And because the image at the back of the large-format cameras was often read on a glass plate, reversed and upside down, vetting it required great concentration. One photographer would test Katie's concentration by adding a random, small object to the shot and challenging her to spot it on the glass plate.

Back at Condé Nast, as assistant to editor Carolyn Sollis, Katie spent countless hours peering through

Katie was an assistant at *House & Garden* when it was reborn as *HG* under Anna Wintour and began to feature models among the furnishings on its covers.

a loupe to identify every fabric in each room on transparencies. The tedious task of recognizing fabrics from their pattern and color on these tiny images yielded an extremely useful skill. Determining which image could convey the spirit of an entire issue was an important moment each month. Alexander Liberman, the renowned Condé Nast editorial director, would gather a few staff members to assess possible covers pinned on the wall. Katie came to see that the skills she learned in the editorial world went some way to making up for her lack of formal training.

When Anna Wintour became editor in chief of *House & Garden* in 1987, the magazine was renamed *HG* and featured models and fashion among the chairs and curtains. Katie recalled that the staff was nervous, and some editors even shortened their skirts and switched from flats to heels. But Katie got along with Anna and was given some good assignments. Instructed to interview a list of younger architects and designers, she visited my office at the Mark Hotel, which my firm was renovating. Though she approved my apartment for photography, the story never ran, but we were engaged six months after the photo shoot.

In 1988 Katie moved to *House Beautiful* as a decorating editor. For each feature, the editors would assign a decorator to tackle a house using the products of a company like IKEA, Baker, or Drexel Heritage, supplemented by decorative accessories and a few antiques. In what she thought of as decorating boot camp, Katie and her team would swoop down on a house that had been volunteered, move the owner's possessions out, install the furnishings, complete the photo shoot, pack up, and return all of the owner's furnishings. The experience of working so closely with so many great talents, like editor Margaret Kennedy, proved invaluable when she began her own decorating firm.

While Katie was observing the world from sunny California, I was growing up in New York City in the gray days of the 1960s and '70s, when thousands of buildings were foreclosed and abandoned, construction was limited, and graffiti and decay were everywhere. But in my neighborhood, there was a certain pride that came with not being one of the many families that had decamped to the suburbs. Having a front row seat to the ravages of urban decay made us feel like citizen activists, though living in a townhouse on East 65th Street was hardly rough. The politics of this period were deeply fraught, but my family was optimistic and engaged politically and socially. My mother taught in a Head Start program; my father served on the boards of the Metropolitan Museum and other civic institutions and, with friends, built a residence for recently released state prisoners.

I found it exciting to accompany my father to the Metropolitan Museum and see the construction of the new wings—the Temple of Dendur, Lehman, and so on—but it was his work as chairman of the Art Commission that really grabbed my attention. This obscure city agency, formed in the late nineteenth century, was an official voice for good design, entrusted with approval of every project built on city-owned land—from a telephone booth to a public school. Unfortunately, in the 1970s there seemed to be little

At *House Beautiful* Katie was an editor for stories like this one that featured furniture available at retail. Ethereal balloon shades were in fashion.

In the 1980s Peter's firm had offices in the Hyde Park Hotel, which they transformed into the Mark. Converting the original apartments into hotel rooms was a great opportunity for the young firm.

Peter grew up in the house with the copper bay at the center of this side street in New York's Upper East Side.

consensus about what constituted good design, but the idea that design could be thought of as more than a private matter stirred my interest in architecture and made me feel as though I was living in a city that was more than a collection of individual buildings.

So while Katie was worrying about the banality of tract housing, I was thinking about the threat of new, soulless architecture to the New York I loved. When the brownstone tenements that lined the end of our block were demolished and replaced by a high-rise apartment tower, I was stricken. I didn't know what a new building should look like, but I did know that one of my favorites, the Plaza Hotel, was closer to what should have been. My eighth-grade essay comparing the two was my first preservation protest.

I found inspiration and encouragement in my family's circle of friends. Our next-door neighbor, Jacques Guiton, a modernist who came to New York from France after World War II, worked with Gordon Bunshaft on the design of the 1961 glass-and-steel tower for the Chase Manhattan bank near Wall Street. And the white penthouse he built for his family was in dazzling contrast to the faded architecture of his mother-in-law's 1860s townhouse beneath. Jacques was a heroic character to me. Even when he dismissed New York's subways because the stations weren't vaulted, he seemed inspired by optimism. I was also curious to know more about the architect he revered named Le Corbusier, whom I would later come to see as a totalitarian.

Charles Platt, the grandson of the architect of the Freer Gallery of Art in Washington, D.C., designed a sprawling white clapboard house in a Bauhaus-meets-New-England-farmhouse style for my aunt and uncle that was chosen as a Record House of the Year by *Architectural Record* magazine. I was fascinated by the plan, which allowed my cousin to enjoy a bedroom lit by a north-facing skylight that would have seemed at home on the sawtooth profile of a factory roof. Inspired by Platt and Guiton, I would spend hours drawing ruled perspectives of imaginary International Style streetscapes that, in hindsight, must have had all of the charm of a suburban office park.

Remaining in New York, I attended Columbia College, where the architect Robert A. M. Stern was making waves by questioning the orthodoxy of modernism. As an acolyte of the architect Robert Venturi and architectural historian Vincent Scully at Yale, Stern was challenging the way history had been dismissed by the academic architectural establishment. His scholarship, his advocacy of the relevance of history, his love of old buildings, and his commitment to New York made him a compelling figure. As a freshman, I knew that I wanted to be an architect but decided that I would start my studio courses in graduate school so that I could devote my undergraduate years to my major, French literature. Bob, whom I had met socially, convinced me otherwise. He insisted that I should be drawing and studying architecture as a preparation for graduate studies and that his studio course was the place to start.

The student body rated his Junior Studio the most difficult class in the undergraduate curriculum—none could approach its rigor and demands. At the outset, Bob explained that we would be very busy and said he hoped no one had a girlfriend or boyfriend because we wouldn't have time to see them and that if anyone thought they had time to commute they should find a place to sleep on campus. Complete commitment to the course was mandatory. Three students dropped out in the first three weeks.

Our first assignment was to create accurate plans and elevations of a historic house based on little more than small, indistinct plans and views published in old journals. Preparing my drawings of an obscure Frank Lloyd Wright house forced me to reconstruct the house, dimension by dimension, making each element fit into the overall scheme in size, scale, and proportion. From the old, fuzzy published plan and elevation, I had to extrapolate the principles of Wright's design in order to build the parts that were missing or unclear. What Bob had us doing was a new version of a staple in the curriculum of the august École des Beaux-Arts in Paris. The rigor of this assignment made it one of the many valuable lessons that I learned that year and would continue to learn as a student and employee of Bob Stern.

Another assignment was to design a branch library, an exercise that required an understanding of the buildings flanking the site—a Brooklyn street built in the 1880s. Drawing my design to relate to its neighbors—even aligning the cornice and height

A rendering of Robert A. M. Stern Architects' Biennale Façade for the *Strada Novissima* installation at the 1980 Venice Biennale. Peter worked at the firm during the heyday of postmodernism.

Peter drew this design for a branch library on a site in historic Cobble Hill, Brooklyn, for an assignment in an undergraduate studio.

to make my library part of the streetscape—I discovered that I could make my imaginary building part of the real city, at least on paper.

After graduating from Columbia College, I worked at Bob Stern's office—then a mere eight-employee firm—sorting slides and helping with exhibit designs and small apartment renovations. When I entered the graduate school at Columbia, I kept my connection to "the office," as those who were working and studying at the same time called it. This experience provided the training that enabled me to go out on my own with Peter Moore, a classmate. Continuing this challenging balance, we started our fledgling studio while still in graduate school. Most of our initial projects were small loft renovations. We were soon joined by Gregory Gilmartin and Thomas Nugent, who work with me to this day.

In 1987, when I met Katie on her editorial assignment, my firm was fully immersed in the renovation of the Mark Hotel, where our client, Bill Judson, had allowed us to set up our office. From the start, it was clear that Katie and I came at design from opposite sides of the table. Whereas she valued informality and color, I was into classicism and dim tones.

Though we lived a mere five blocks from each other, visiting was like going to a different country—even a different climate. A lime-green sofa with chintz pillows dominated Katie's living room. Light pine consoles were the darkest pieces of furniture in the place. It was a sun-filled, white-walled paean to the good life in a warm locale—Pebble Beach, perhaps. It had such an uplifting, welcoming atmosphere that the view east to Third Avenue and its jumbled roofscapes seemed incongruous.

My apartment, on the other hand, was dark and cramped. In the small living room I had built partitions and cabinetry and panels in an attempt to instill the spirit of Sir John Soane, Thomas Jefferson, a little bit of Stern, and God knows who else. The walls were cream and dark maroon with black trim. The floors were black vinyl tile with brass inlays. It resembled nothing so much as the tight quarters of a collector's cabinet.

Even the details of our professional assignments suggest that opposites do indeed attract. While Katie was producing a story about a bright, airy beach house, my firm was proposing a monotone *analytique* drawing for the outside wall of the offices of Andy Warhol's *Interview* magazine, complete with a reliquary for Brigid Berlin's pugs beneath.

The first project we collaborated on was the creation of a store. It was instigated, strangely enough, by a compromise on a vacation destination. Katie wanted to be in the sun, preferably on a beach, while I was angling for London or—as Katie put it—to be in the rain in a city. Somehow we settled on Istanbul. Katie thought she knew the marketplace for fabrics and decorative accessories from her work at the magazines, but

Peter's firm created the Mark Bar in the late 1980s, just steps away from their office on the fourth floor of the Mark Hotel. The location made it a perfect room for meetings.

Peter's bachelor apartment featured black cabinetry displaying plaster casts, alabaster urns, books, and prints. The center table was painted to match the Biedermeier furniture.

she was dazzled by unexpected finds in the Grand Bazaar and the museum shops. She discovered that the great tradition of Iznik ceramics—the height of artistic achievement in the Ottoman Empire—had inspired exquisite fabrics and tiles, none of which were available in the U.S.

Upon our return, we quickly researched ways to import the goods and learned that we would be able to order fabrics that were produced for the Istanbul Archaeology Museums. The store, Katie Ridder Home Furnishings, which I helped design and stock, was located on Lexington Avenue just four blocks from my childhood home.

The store proved popular among decorators and people in the worlds of fashion and design. Katie enjoyed introducing fabrics and wares that had never been seen in the U.S. before, and our buying trips were a great chance for us to collaborate and test each other's instincts on what would appeal to New Yorkers, as well as to understand each other's taste.

Looking back on those early days now, we agree that it was what we didn't have in common that most intrigued each of us. I found Katie's penchant for clear, vivid colors invigorating and warm—an antidote to the introspection fostered by a dark interior. She found that the structure and detail of my work—its solid composure—dispelled the visual instability of some of the modernist architecture she encountered in her work as an editor. What bound our taste together was a common interest in learning and evolving in our work. Neither of us, to this day, believes that there is a final, perfect resolution to our aesthetic differences. Both of us are still learning.

Our initial steps toward a common vision were a bit tentative. But when we were decorating our first apartment on West 77th Street, across from the Museum of Natural History, I had an epiphany about color. I happened to visit a modernist house, the owner of which had begged for color, and the architect had reluctantly agreed that one wall could be green. I embraced the idea, and Katie chose a bright, intense blue for the west wall of our living room. She understood that it would add depth to the room and make a sound backdrop for my varied and mismatched collection of prints, paintings, and photography.

We now refer to this period as the staple-and-glue-gun phase of our marriage. We were constantly transforming things in ways that were effective for our own apartment but that we would never have recommended for a client. Our dining room was filled with choice pieces of our loot from Turkey. Katie glued an Anatolian camel saddlebag fringe with bushy woolen tassels around the doorframe. A mosque lantern hovered above the dining room table, and a "mouse trap" (a ceramic orb element used in suspending oil lamps) hung in front of our window bay. I painted the cheerful country pine consoles from Katie's first apartment black, and I designed and cut a stencil in a Greek key motif to apply to the apron of the tables in gold paint.

The black tables may have been my last rebellion, as Katie soon realized that I could enjoy color too. Our first car was a 1963 Buick Special that Keith Haring painted for my firm in partial

TOP A mosque lantern found at the Grand Bazaar in Istanbul hung over the couple's dining room table in their first apartment. They chose to use tea candles instead of the traditional oil. CENTER A reproduction cast-iron urn was among the offerings at Katie's store. Merchandise that didn't move, like this urn, would often find its way into the couple's apartment. ABOVE Katie on a buying trip in Istanbul in 1990. The architecture, decorative arts, and atmosphere of Turkey were exotic and inspiring.

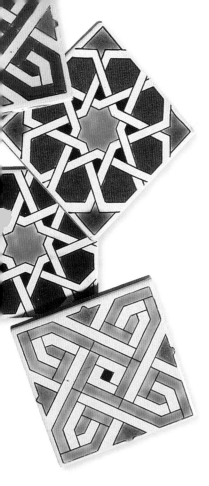

Katie's store was an ever-changing gallery of objects that she and Peter found on their travels. Set up like a living room, the store offered reproductions, newly made traditional crafts, fabrics and tiles, and antiques. BELOW Katie was photographed among her wares for a feature in *New York* magazine. CLOCKWISE FROM TOP LEFT Geometric hand-painted tiles from Turkey; a reproduction classical urn; a "mouse trap"—a glazed ceramic orb traditionally used on a chandelier chain to thwart thirsty mice from drinking the oil in mosque lanterns; a brass lantern made by traditional craftsmen along modern lines; an inlaid Syrian-style armoire used to display exotic finds, ranging from silvered bathhouse soapboxes to cricket cages from China; the store's sofa, popular with designers and friends who came to browse and stayed to talk; rolls of traditional dress fabric from a supplier in the Grand Bazaar, used in Turkey to made country dresses but in New York a one-time popular choice for upholstery and, for one customer, a perfect material for slippers; an intricate lantern with screenlike panels made in Egypt, a typical example of Katie's approach to finding a common object in a special form.

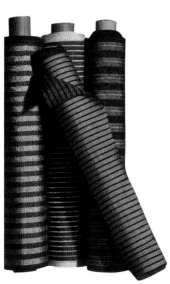

In their first apartment, Katie painted one wall blue as a backdrop for Peter's collection of prints, including the twelve-foot-long baroque reconstruction of the Baths of Caracalla.

Camel saddlebag fringe and a line of starfish framed the entrance to the dining room. Turkish chargers mounted on the wall and overscale tureens complete the eccentric decoration.

payment for my design of his store, the Pop Shop, in SoHo. And she also made me see that contrast was a virtue in creating a good interior—that traditional architecture didn't require period furniture and that sharp colors could make you see art and objects in a different light.

When Katie began decorating professionally, she closed her store, and this new chapter in her career allowed us to work in close collaboration on a number of extraordinary projects. Among our favorites was the total rebuilding and decoration of an Italianate farmhouse in the hunt country of Virginia. My firm documented the history of this much-diminished 1850s farmhouse villa, finding evidence of original moldings and architectural features like bay windows. Based on this research, we added features that had never been built but were inspired by the original pattern book. While we were re-creating our version of Italianate architecture, Katie set about incorporating the client's old family furniture and art into a more youthful design with bright color and more contemporary furnishings. The highlights of the project, we agreed, were those places where our individual contributions combined to reinforce our respective strengths and the overall design.

Keith Haring painted Peter's 1963 Buick Special after his firm completed the artist's studio and Pop Shop. Haring had offered Peter a painting, but his white car proved to be an irresistible canvas.

At the center of a historic Virginia villa, in what had been a dark stair hall, Peter's firm designed a cupola framed by an oculus ornamented with anthemia and oak leaves.

In the stair hall, for example, typically a darker space in the villa plan because it has no exposures, my firm added a circular opening in the ceiling, topped by a large cupola that brought in light from all sides. Katie's response to this flood of daylight was brilliant orange wallpaper by Zuber.

As our practices grew, we took on projects that allowed us to integrate artisanship at a level that we could have only dreamed of before. For a project in San Francisco, we collaborated on a renovation that encompassed sculptural bas-relief, painted effects, and salvaged antique ceilings. In one powder room, on walls Katie had painted a glossy apple green, I proposed a grid of Sèvres porcelain flowers. As these ornaments weren't available in the quantity that the design required, Katie worked with an artist to have them formed of sheet metal and painted to look botanically correct.

At this stage we found that our essentially different tastes inspired rather than limited our design ideas. We were at our most open and imaginative when working together. A conversation might start with the thought that we should consider bas-relief for the walls of a dining room rather than straight paint or wallpaper. By the time we settled on a design—in this case a bas-relief of an imaginary land where an egret

OPPOSITE In the stair hall below the cupola, Katie chose a rich orange Zuber wallpaper and an Oushak carpet that reflected the warm light of the space.

For a powder room in San Francisco, Katie commissioned a variety of hand-painted metal flowers that she set against glossy apple-green walls. Peter's classical sink base featured a Greek key.

stands on one leg amid flora inspired by the fabrics of Josef Frank—we couldn't remember and really didn't care who had come up with the idea first.

Though for the most part I worked with other decorators, including Albert Hadley, Jeffrey Bilhuber, and, very often, Thomas Jayne, we still had clients who wanted both my firm's architecture and Katie's decoration. The contrast between my rather studied interior architecture and Katie's looser, more intuitive decorating style resulted in some of our favorite projects. But Katie was also willing to rein in her vivid color palette and adopt a more reserved approach when the project involved restoration. While I was restoring the nineteenth-century interiors of a townhouse in a historic district in New York, Katie took on the restoration and decoration of a 1930s Japanese pavilion that had been given to the Vanderbilt family by the emperor of Japan. Her painstaking restoration of antique wall-paper panels and woodwork and her choice of a color palette that defers to the historic character of the building would have been exactly my approach given the same opportunity. So in many ways we were learning from each other.

In our house in Bronxville, New York, we were able to fuse our styles seamlessly for the first time, though we still let the range of our individual taste show through. Katie's decoration was becoming bolder, as she was experimenting more. In the entrance, for instance, my great-grandfather's high chair faces a stair rail that she lacquered in candy-apple red with a silver stripe. Her treatment of the living room, however, was more restrained. Using the remaining stock from her store, Katie created an exotic lounge that we dubbed the Zam-Zam room. Here, we chose not to edit at all. We framed the entrance with portieres trimmed with ornamental tape that Katie had found in Salzburg and topped by a Tibetan embroidered pelmet, and we clad the entire fireplace wall in mirror enclosed in Moroccan mosharabi turned-wood lattice panels.

Eventually, we decided to find land for our own country place. For years we had spent part of August on Mishaum Point, in South Dartmouth, Massachusetts, sharing a rambling 1890s Shingle Style house designed by William Ralph Emerson that had belonged to my grandmother. And we had spent almost every

OPPOSITE Following the painstaking restoration of this historic Japanese pavilion, Katie introduced tatami mats stitched together with leather to form the floor covering and lime-green linen curtains.

The living room scheme in Katie and Peter's Bronxville house revolves around the blues and creams found in the antique carpet. A great carpet is often the foundation of Katie's designs.

Christmas with Katie's parents and her family in Hawaii. Sharing the South Dartmouth place with my siblings and their families gave our children an indelible connection to their extended family, but we craved a vacation place of our own.

In 1999 we began looking in earnest up the Hudson River. In Germantown we found a twelve-acre parcel perched on a bluff directly over the river, with Roecliff Jansen Kill, a tributary, to the north. With its sweeping views of the Catskill Mountains across the Hudson, it seemed like a perfect spot for a weekend house. Before I drew the plans, I spent many nights camping with our kids in a tent on the spot where we thought we should build. Since the land offered an oblique view of Frederic Church's house, Olana, which is renowned for its Moorish decorative motifs, I felt justified in clothing the simple, box-shaped villa I designed in ornament inspired by Moorish architecture.

OPPOSITE The Zam-Zam room, a sky-lit lounge in the Bronxville house, is a favorite for kids' parties, some sanctioned and some covert. They found the carpet in Morocco and the lanterns in Istanbul, and Katie designed the bead-fringed ceiling shades.

The commission to design Drumlin Hall near Millbrook was a great opportunity for Peter's firm, and being in the area convinced him of its beauty.

Peter designed a Moorish-inspired villa for a parcel of land in Germantown, New York, that reflected the style of neighboring Olana, Frederick Church's house. Like the Millbrook house, it was a simple boxlike, flat-roofed pavilion.

Though we felt good about the plans for a small three-bedroom house, the site was close enough to the local thoroughfare that we could hear trucks as they geared up and down at the adjacent bridge. Realizing how important the silence of the country was to us, we reluctantly sold the land and resolved that our next search would focus only on areas that were thoroughly agricultural and where truck traffic would be a distant memory.

Finally, in 2009, in the midst of the financial downturn, when we thought there might be some deals to be had, we zeroed in on the area near the village of Millbrook, New York. I had known about Millbrook for years. We had friends who had houses there, and many relatives had attended the Millbrook School. I became more familiar with the area when my firm was hired in 2005 to design a new house near Milbrook. The client's brief—to imagine that the British neoclassical architect Robert Adam and the American cabinetmaker Duncan Phyfe together designed a villa for a lady—made this a dream project for any architect. Led by Gregory Gilmartin and Tom Nugent, our firm produced a compact, classical stone villa that had four symmetrical façades, each a different but related design. The way Gregory created an architectural response to the views, relating each major room to the area of the landscape it looked out on, made me realize the potential of an open site in the rolling landscape of the Hudson River Valley. And the better we came to know the area, the more convinced we were that we could find land for a house in Millbrook.

✳

A HOUSE IN
THE COUNTRY

A TAPESTRY OF TILLED FIELDS, PASTURES, AND WOODS, DUTCHESS COUNTY, IN THE SOUTHEAST corner of New York State, retains much of its historic agrarian flavor and natural beauty. And Millbrook—the jewel-like village in the town of Washington—has become something of a catchall for the surrounding towns and hamlets, as well as a moniker that communicates the spirit and essence of the place. Life in Millbrook is very much tied to the land. Agriculture and equestrian activities have spared the area the deforestation that comes with suburban development, and wide swaths of farmland and forest remain untouched. The area has a down-to-earth grit grounded in its crop, dairy, and cattle farms, but its history as a fashionable getaway for New Yorkers gives it a certain old-school glamour. Though the atmosphere is low-key, the traditional sporting pursuits of fox hunting, horseback riding, polo, fishing, and shooting are important to the life of the community.

Historically, farming was the economic basis of the area, as the land was both fertile and convenient to the Hudson River, where shipping provided access to the New York markets. What began as a Quaker settlement in the 1700s grew into a fashionable retreat in the second half of the nineteenth century. Several Quaker families, some still prominent in the area, accumulated wealth and built large houses. In 1850 Jonathan Thorne, who had made a fortune in leather manufacturing, transformed an older house into Thorndale, now a Millbrook landmark. And other local Quakers—particularly John D. Wing, a successful soda ash manufacturer—began attracting friends to the area. New, expansive, architect-designed houses with distinctive names such as Altamont, Sandanona, Edgewood, and Daheim began rising on the rolling hills around the village of Millbrook, which was officially incorporated in 1896. Halcyon Hall, a colossal luxury hotel developed in the 1890s, promoted Millbrook's scenery to a wider public, promising visitors the "softness of Devonshire and Surrey landscapes" and a "horizon outlined by billowy mountains and serrated peaks."

More recently, horse farms and specialty farms have reinvigorated the area. Since 1985, the Dutchess Land Conservancy has successfully preserved more than 39,000 acres of farmland, wildlife habitats, and scenic views, and various sporting and fishing preserves, including the Tamarack Preserve, the Mashomack Fish and Game Preserve, and the Orvis Sandanona Shooting Grounds, have secured the use of open land, perpetuating its use for sport. Traditional English foxhunting is still celebrated by the Millbrook Hunt, founded in 1907. As one of the top equestrian organizations in the country, it plays a vital role in the community as a steward of land conservation and open space. The appeal and tradition of Millbrook lie in its land. Families

---

View of the west façade from the far side of the pond.

long entrenched in the community, newly arrived weekenders, farmers, and sportsmen alike uphold this reverence for nature.

Though not horse people themselves—Katie is allergic—it was this landscape that drew Katie and Peter to Millbrook. They'd been thinking of building a getaway for years. However, the search for a site was complicated. Peter didn't want to infringe on historic land uses by building on a division of a farm field—that seemed to run counter to the spirit of Millbrook—and the landscape would feel raw and new. Nor did he want to clear the old-growth forest on a wooded site. Rather, he decided to focus on properties already occupied by a house—he had learned in his architectural practice that the mature trees of an established site offer a new house a more plausible and resonant connection to the land. In 2009 he and Katie finally found the perfect parcel—six and a half acres on a rise, accessed along an old dirt road, with views of a lake and hills in the distance. Close to one of the area's thoroughfares but not on a main road, its location at the intersection of two less-traveled roads and its relatively level grade made it a typical corner lot for a farmhouse. Peter suspected it had long been the site of a house, and his excavator did indeed uncover a nineteenth-century foundation. At the time, though, it was home to a one-story 1960s ranch house that had languished on the market for two years. There was a paddock for horses, a muddy and boggy pond, and a 1980s aluminum-sided barn with a four-bay garage, six horse stalls, a tack room, and a two-bedroom apartment. All of these elements were strung in a line on a long, narrow site—just 195 feet wide at its narrowest, but 810 feet long from east to west. That one generous dimension meant that the site felt paradoxically large. There was room for Peter and Katie to create a whole series of events—lawn, house and garden, parking court, pond, grove, and meadow—on the long axis of the site. But possibly the best feature of the parcel was that it was surrounded by fields of rotating crops—corn, beans, and hay—making the skinny site feel open and expansive as well as private. With the Tamarack Preserve and Rally Farms—a

The Benham Farm in the town of Washington, New York, ca. 1900–1920.

The Millbrook Hunt on the terrace at Edgewood, ca. 1920.

2,400-acre pure-bred Angus farm—as neighbors, the site was located in the heart of Millbrook's hunt country, and various friends from New York—including Fernanda Kellogg and Kirk Henckels of Fitch's Corner, a private equestrian facility—were nearby. It was an ideal spot for Peter and Katie to design a house together and for Katie, a garden enthusiast of some twenty years, to establish a garden.

Katie and Peter had their work cut out for them. They spent almost two years improving the site while planning the new house. For some time, the land had suffered at the hands of unbridled nature. Poison ivy flourished in the hedgerows, grapevines had overtaken the trees, and algae and weeds had clogged the pond at the center of the property, turning it into a fetid bog. But as Peter and Katie restored the landscape, they discovered new vistas, and the site itself seemed to grow larger. They brought in Roy Budnick, a local environmental engineer, to restore and expand the pond. Now a half acre in extent and eighteen feet deep, the pond is fed by a stream running from the south and teems with bullfrogs, turtles, ducks, and muskrats—plus one vigilant egret that waits daily to spear one of the carp or koi that Katie has imported from a local fishery. As they cleared the land, they also experienced the north wind well known to the locals—a force funneled from the lake and valley below, its imprint borne out by the patterns of the snowdrifts in the winter. But to Katie and Peter, being stationed on an exposed plain was a good thing; they agreed that a perfect view of land should also include the spectacle of dramatic weather.

✳

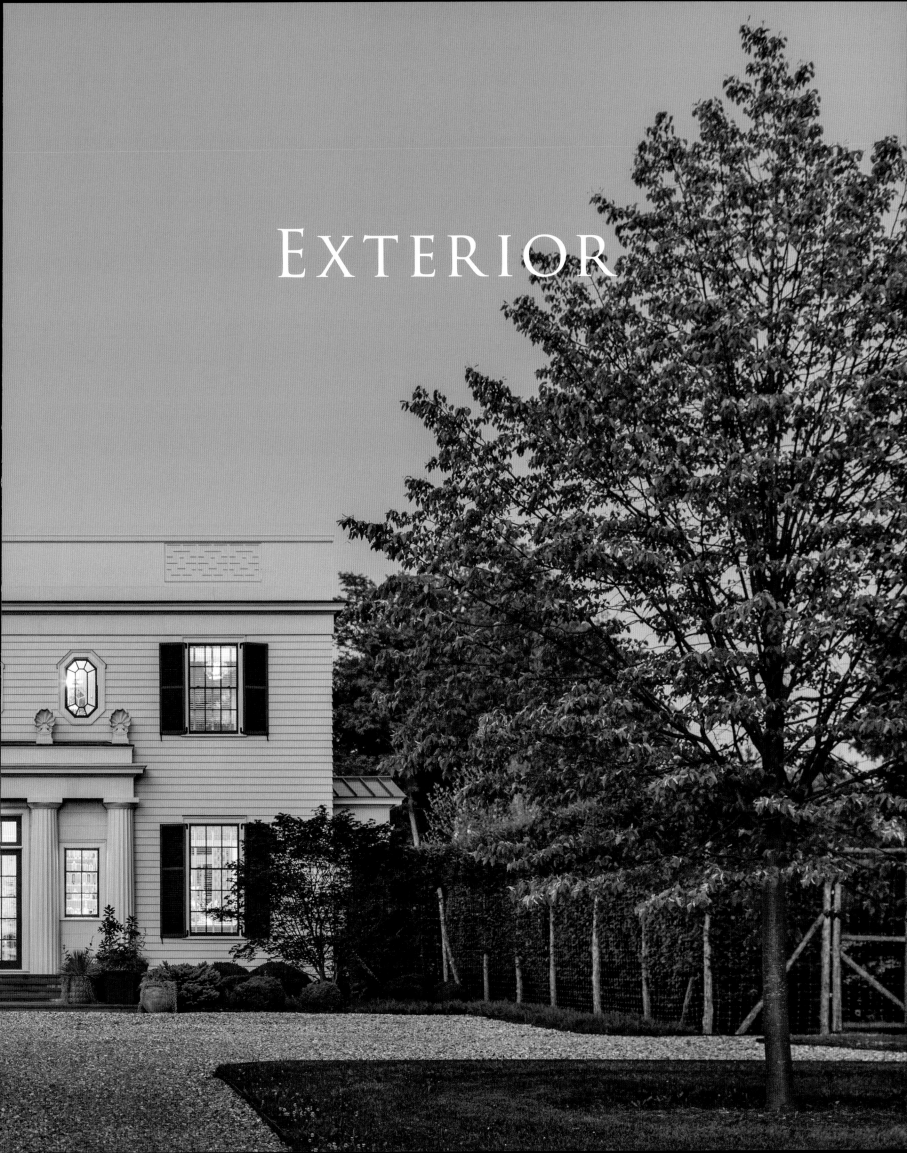

EXTERIOR

As soon as they were in contract on the place, Peter and Katie discovered that they could tell what their views from the second floor would be like by standing on the roof of the old house. Aside from being stranded when he went up alone and the ladder fell over, Peter found this a useful exercise. Indeed, it confirmed the fact that the ranch house was well positioned to take advantage of the best views, so Peter and Katie chose to build on the same spot.

After years of thinking about houses and building them for clients, Peter had an idea of what he wanted for his own house. "From the first time I ever sketched a house," he recalls, "it had always been a simple box with a flat roof." This remained a constant even as his sense of style evolved and matured over the years. His catalogue of unbuilt works includes several examples of this "architect's cube." In the 1980s, when he co-owned land in Wainscott, New York, he'd designed a rectangular villa decorated with urns on its cornice. He called it Cinder House because of its concrete-block walls. Later, when he and Katie were thinking of building in Germantown, New York, farther up the Hudson, he'd designed another flat-roofed villa, this one enhanced with Moorish details inspired by Frederic Church's house, Olana, a local landmark. By the time Millbrook came along, Peter's thoughts had turned to the Greek Revival.

For the design of the house, he collaborated with Gregory Gilmartin, his longtime colleague and friend, who channeled Peter's vision of an architect's cube. Peter had sketched some ideas that were fundamental to the plan: he wanted open rooms and built-in cabinets for storing the various artifacts that he and Katie had collected, as well as a double-height space distinct from the stair hall. He also showed Gregory a photograph from *Maine Forms of American Architecture*, a book he'd owned since high school, of a house that had entranced him ever since—the Jonas Cutting–Edward Kent House in Bangor, designed around 1833 by Charles G. Bryant. Bryant combined Greek Doric columns, colossal piers, deep reveals, and cast-iron grilles in the attic windows to create a stylish, flat-roofed double house for a pair of law partners. Meant as an inspiration rather than as a model to copy, the house in Bangor demonstrated how a wooden Greek Revival house could take on more architectural character. It was vernacular and classical, humble and monumental. Too monumental even: the two-story piers fronting Penobscot Street in Bangor would have seemed out of place rising out of Millbrook's farm fields. Having worked with Peter for more than thirty years, Gregory knew the full range of his tastes. He infused the design with a broader set of references—from Karl Friedrich Schinkel, Sir John Soane, Delano & Aldrich, and Duncan

---

PRECEDING PAGES The west façade. With four fluted Greek Doric columns capped by deeply sculpted palmette ornaments, or acroteria, this is the most formal elevation of the house. ABOVE One of the acroteria topping the columns that front the west façade. OPPOSITE The first view of the house is the south façade rising across the pastures.

Katie surveys the views from the roof of the existing ranch house.

Phyfe to Benjamin Latrobe—and combined these with his own sense of elegance and grace. Peter felt that the result was a testament to their years of creative collaboration.

As completed, the house is a perfectly resolved box with four distinct, symmetrical façades that belie the programmatic complexities within. To achieve a harmonious resolution between the exterior, the interior plan, and the garden required that the design be developed simultaneously in plan, section, and elevation. The first sight of the house is of the southern façade rising across the open fields. This is the simplest façade of the house, giving it the appearance of little more than a clapboard box—or rather a refined farmhouse with a one-story, pedimented and pilastered projection housing the mudroom. The east façade parallels the road, and the somewhat heavy Greek Revival piers of its porch and the regular rhythm of the parapet railings lend the house a generous scale. As you turn left onto the dirt road, the north façade comes into view, and the house suddenly takes on the character of a neoclassical villa. A semicircular bay with whimsical bas-reliefs depicting a dog chasing a rabbit between its pilasters breaks forward from the wall. Reminiscent of details in the work of Delano & Aldrich, the bas-reliefs immortalize Teddy, Peter and Katie's dachshund, and were sculpted by Abigail Tulis, a graduate of the Grand Central Academy and the Beaux-Arts Atelier. Two more right-angled turns bring you to the west façade and front door—the most formal elevation and something of a stylistic manifesto. Three octagonal casements enhance the second floor; below them, a frontispiece of four fluted Doric columns announces the main entrance. The elevation resembles the front of Oak Knoll in Mill Neck, New York, one of Peter's favorite Delano & Aldrich houses, and of another "architect's cube"—Pitzhanger Manor, Sir John Soane's own country villa in West London. At Pitzhanger, four columns support sculpted priestesses, but here they are crowned by acroteria—deeply sculpted palmette ornaments—designed by Gregory and modeled on the computer by Tim Kelly, representing the columns budding into new life. Above the cornice line, a parapet detailed with fretwork masks a low-sloped roof, giving the impression of that flat-roofed house Peter had always dreamed of. To soften the classical façades, Katie chose to paint the exterior a warm gray, enlivened by cherry-red

The 1833 Jonas Cutting–Edward Kent House in Bangor, Maine, which Peter had admired since college. Its boxlike simplicity and carved-wood classical details were a key inspiration.

window sashes and deep blue shutters. As Peter said, "We didn't want it to be just another white Greek Revival house."

And it is not. At first glance, from a distance, the wood-framed house with clapboard siding may appear to be old, comfortably nestled in its Millbrook landscape for generations. But the generous size and consistent proportions of many details—in particular the windows, the bombé north side, and the overall symmetries—make it clear that the house is new. Outwardly traditional, the house also represents the best of current building practices and materials, especially in terms of energy performance. Peter has always believed that traditional design, evolved long before the use of fossil fuels for heating and cooling, is inherently "green." Porches that offer shade in summer but admit the low-angled

TOP The Delano & Aldrich–designed apartment house where Peter lived when he first met Katie sported this whimsical frieze of tortoises and hares. Delano's design inspired the frieze of dachshunds and a rabbit on the north façade of the Millbrook house. ABOVE A tortoise fountain designed by Peter's firm for a client. The firm has long included sculpture in its projects.

sun in the winter, double-hung windows that allow natural convection through the upper sash, and a large chimney mass at the center of the plan are all direct, traditional responses to the environment. Peter eschewed LEED certification, a noble goal complicated by bureaucracy and fees, but the house was built to the highest energy-efficiency standards. Meeting this goal was the task of a team in Peter's office who developed the construction drawings and specifications; Jim Taylor, one of Peter's partners, supervised the work of associates Matthew Cummings, Cecilia Rodgers, Arthur Rollin, Tim Kelly, and John Gibbons. Thick wall framing provided the depth for both soy-based spray and conventional batt insulation—almost doubling the amount of insulation of a typical house. Advantech, a proprietary sheathing system, and rainscreen cladding made the building envelope very tight—important on such a windy site—and a high-efficiency boiler, radiant Warmboard heat distributed from an impressed layer of aluminum under all the floors, and LED lighting further enhanced the house's performance. All of the mechanical systems, from thermostats to the television, can be controlled remotely by a swipe on a phone.

The small garage off of the entrance court is deliberately understated so it would not compete with the house. Jim Taylor specified lime stucco as a finish rather than the now-ubiquitous elastomeric coating, ensuring that the structure would age naturally, hairline cracks and all. When Colin Calhoun, the contractor's

TOP Sir John Soane's Pitzhanger Manor inspired the column screen and acroteria on the west façade of the house. ABOVE Oak Knoll, an elegant classical villa in Mill Neck, New York, was designed by Delano & Aldrich. Its flat roof, symmetry, and the architectural interest of its center bay served as an inspiration for the Millbrook house.

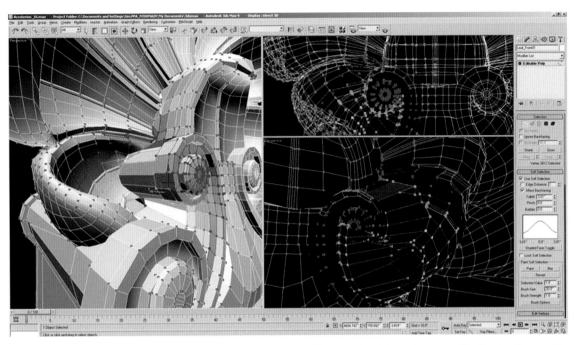

ABOVE A screen shot of the 3D modeling of the prototype acroterion. This digital model was then printed by Peter's office, providing a maquette for the sculpting of the full-scale version. OVERLEAF Site plan.

foreman, offered two inexpensive windows that another Westerley Construction client had rejected, Peter snapped them up and incorporated them into the back wall of the building. Inside, the walls were sheathed in moisture-resistant sheetrock backed by plywood—the perfect wall system for mounting and bolting things—and the ceiling was made high to accommodate the pulley system Peter designed to raise a canoe up under the roof.

Squared to the east–west hedgerow running along the town border, the house is perfectly oriented to the points on a compass. Katie's flower garden abuts the southern façade and extends to the southern property line, while most of their land, as well as the dirt lane off of which it is situated, stretches to the west, where cornfields mark the beginning of the neighboring farm. Along this western boundary, a broad grass path bears the imprint of the many hoofs left by the horses bearing the traditionally clad riders of the Millbrook Hunt on their passage south. Because of the way the house is sited, the approach to it takes you around it before you reach the front door. As a result, it seems to rotate: each façade is revealed sequentially. The first view, from across the fields, is of the vernacular south façade, followed by the more conventional east façade with its porch. On the dirt road, you pass the more dynamic bombé north façade and finally, after curving up the driveway, past the pond, you arrive at the classical west façade.

✳

SITE PLAN

1. House   2. Flower Garden   3. Woodland Garden   4. Fire Pit Terrace   5. Pond   6. Cutting Garden   7. Barn

PAGES 48–49 A garden path, flanked by billowing shrubs and flowers, leads south from the mudroom door. The mudroom reads as a small temple, complete with engaged pilasters. PRECEDING PAGES The porch on the east façade has an unusually high (twelve-foot) ceiling to allow sunlight to reach the east-facing rooms. New London plane trees (*Platanus × acerifolia*) soften the view of the house. OPPOSITE Steps lead from the east porch down to the lawn. ABOVE Katie combined simple rattan furniture with vintage folding teak chairs to furnish the porch. Pots of geraniums and gardenias are transferred from the greenhouse in the spring. OVERLEAF Farm fields unfold to the south.

PRECEDING PAGES View of the house from the northeast. ABOVE Abigail Tulis's bas-reliefs fit within the frieze panels above the north-facing bay. Building the curved moldings and siding was a major challenge for the millworkers. OPPOSITE Katie chose a vivid red for the window sashes and the doors and a deep, dark blue for the shutters. OVERLEAF The north façade, bathed in early morning light at the height of autumn.

ABOVE AND OPPOSITE The formal west façade is the front entrance to the house.

ABOVE Red maples, boxwood, and other shrubs soften the west façade and its columns. OPPOSITE A bronze snapping turtle guards the entrance. OVERLEAF The bog at the center of the property was expanded into a half-acre pond that is eighteen feet deep and teeming with wildlife.

PRECEDING PAGES View of the west façade from the far side of the pond. OPPOSITE Peter enjoys trimming the trees and bushes in the woodland garden and along the hedgerows. ABOVE The lower limbs of a gnarled old tree were trimmed to allow a view of the pond beyond. OVERLEAF View of the house from the southeast, amid trees ablaze in autumn colors. Katie chose blue for the roofs of the porch and pediment. PAGES 74–75 The house enveloped in winter flurries.

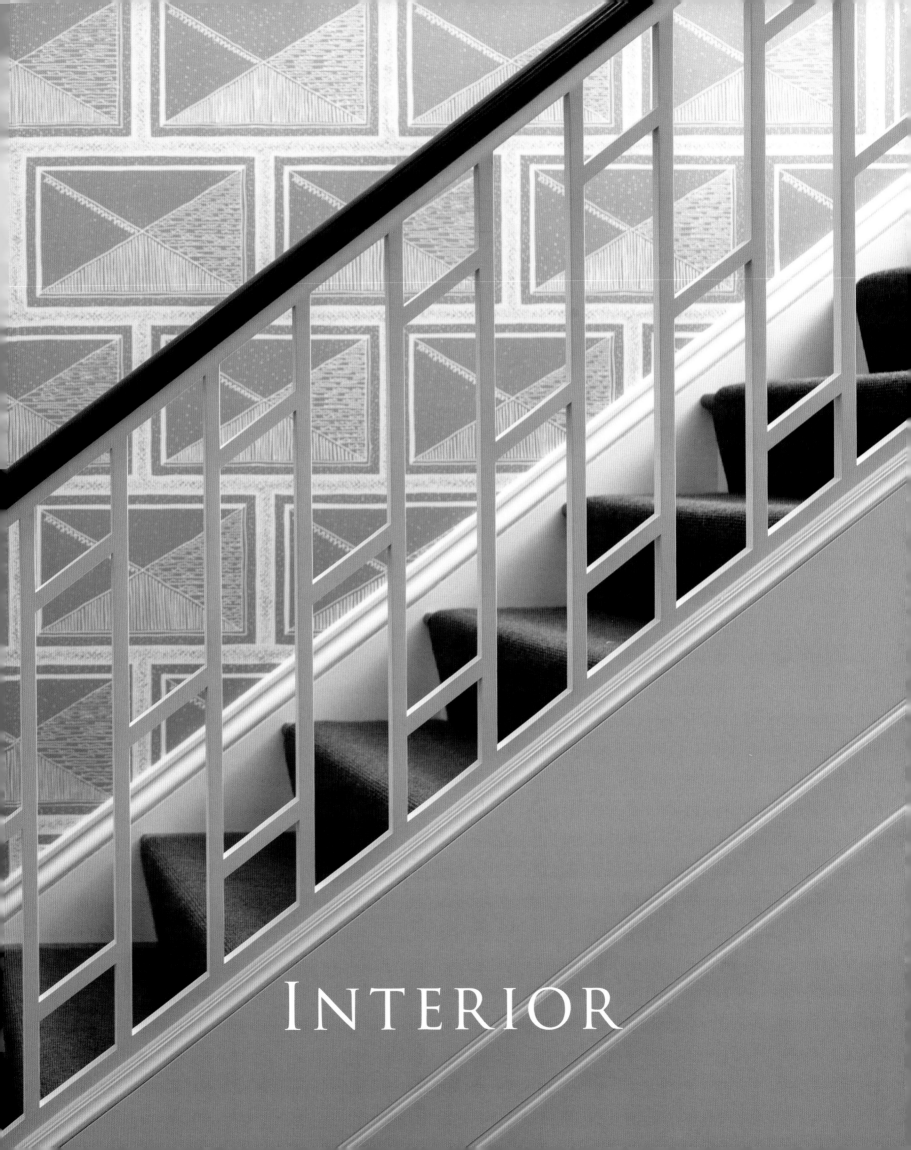

INTERIOR

THE INTERIOR OF THE HOUSE IS BRIGHT AND OPEN, QUALITIES INTENSIFIED BY KATIE'S VIVID color scheme and the absolute precision of the plan. "If you stand in the middle of the house," Peter notes, "you can see daylight in four directions." And, sure enough, from the center point of both the first and second floors, you can see views to the north, south, east, and west. The plan of the house revolves around two axes: the east–west axis extends from the front door through the entrance hall into the living room and out to the porch. The north–south axis runs from the stair hall through the front hall, kitchen, mudroom, and garden to the south gate leading to the fields beyond. All of the rooms are symmetrical and have been slotted into a rectangular footprint behind corresponding symmetrical façades. However difficult this was to achieve, its resolution—with views interwoven from room to room and enfilades of spaces materializing almost magically—feels natural and inevitable. The play between the plan and the façades—a puzzle akin to the complexity of a Rubik's Cube—is solved in seamless simplicity.

Katie and Peter both wanted an open-floor plan with interconnecting rooms. With two children out of the house and only one still at home, they knew there would be times when just the two of them would be in residence. Despite the traditional exterior design, the interiors are modern, intimate, and open. On the first floor, with the exception of the study, powder room, and mudroom, none of the rooms can be entirely closed off with doors, and the entry hall, stair hall, living room, dining room, and kitchen all flow into one another. None of these rooms is very big, but the vistas from one room to another make the house seem more spacious than it is. The smaller spaces like the bar, powder room, and bedroom vestibules received the same amount of architectural attention as the larger rooms because, according to Peter, "The smaller the space, the more carefully articulated it needs to be." As a result, each room feels distinct yet connected, something Katie took into account as her color scheme modulates from one room to the next.

For the main colors, Katie gravitated toward pinks and purples, shades she doesn't normally use in her designs for clients. The reds, blues, yellows, and greens she mixed into the rooms in varying degrees add a layer of complexity, allowing the rooms to interact even more dynamically. Though she worked from a furniture plan, the exact selections were often a matter of serendipity. Because she and Peter relied heavily on auction houses—where they found exciting, unexpected choices and some very good values—the interiors are an array of antiques mixed in with newer pieces. Collections that Peter has accumulated over time—many of which reflect his interest in history—add yet another layer to the mix.

✳

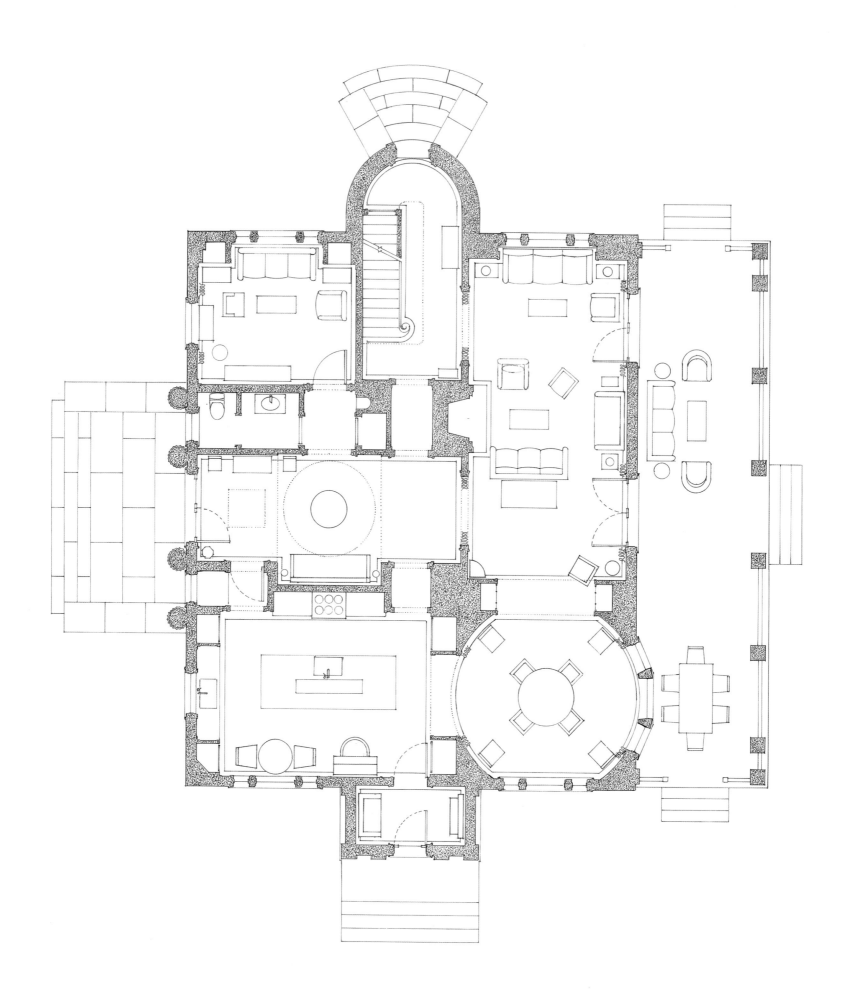

FIRST-FLOOR PLAN

FRONT HALL

IN A TRADITIONAL GREEK REVIVAL OR COLONIAL HOUSE, THE STAIR IS TYPICALLY LOCATED IN THE FRONT hall. Here, however, the double-height space of the hall is completely open to a large, square laylight above the second floor that brings unobstructed light into the center of the house. The hall's generous scale and brightness is striking and unexpected, at once declaring that this house is, indeed, the house of an architect. The loftiness of the space is intensified by vaults: a west vault—with an aperture to bring in additional oblique light from above—mirrors the east vault, which articulates the entrance to the living room and the axis running between the stair hall and the kitchen. At the center, a circular opening at the level of the second-floor balcony slices through the top of the hall's handkerchief dome and frames the square laylight above. Peter had tried out this concept before, in the first house he ever built. Completed in 1990, it was commissioned by the author Louis Auchincloss and his wife, Adele, in Claryville, New York, and it features a

---

PAGES 76–77 Detail of the stair hall, the walls of which are covered in Katie's Scraffito, a paper she designed expressly for the space. PRECEDING PAGES, LEFT Detail of the ikat fabric that covers the sofa in the entrance hall. PRECEDING PAGES, RIGHT Glazed doors with transoms flood the entrance with western light. An opening in the vault above offers a view of the second floor. OPPOSITE First-floor plan. ABOVE View of the front hall from the second floor through the broad, circular opening between the floors. Katie first saw Moroccan mosaic tiles on a trip to Fez. Here she covered the floor with hexagonal tiles in a range of purple shades.

circular opening above Auchincloss's first-floor study that brings in light from a window in the second-floor library. In his design for the Milbrook entrance hall, Gregory Gilmartin marshaled the language of classicism into a fully developed architecture; roundels and busts from Peter's collection, overlooking the hall, animate the space. Much as in Sir John Soane's house in London, objects are both displayed in and enveloped by the architecture.

Because she knew she would be using a lot of color throughout the house, Katie opted for a more neutral palette in the front hall, with the exception of the variegated purple mosaic tile—an element she wanted to use from the get-go. Her affinity for Moroccan tile was initially sparked by a trip to Fez fifteen years ago, but she'd never had the chance to use the purple variety. The hall's glass doors bring in light that not only adds to the tile's lustrous sheen but also highlights Peter's collection of photographs, etchings, and drawings of historic New York City views by such photographers and artists as Alfred Stieglitz, Jessie Tarbox Beals, Thurman Rotan, Martin Lewis, and Joseph Pennell. Here and throughout the house, Peter's firm designed the hardware, which was first hand drawn, then modeled on a 3D printer in his office, and manufactured by Lowe Hardware in Rockport, Maine. On the first floor, doorknobs are engraved with a star motif and finished in copper, while on the second floor, they are modeled after a seedpod-like design that Peter and Katie had seen in Sweden.

ABOVE LEFT Peter's firm designed the hardware for the house, which was executed by Lowe Hardware. On the ground floor he used a star motif on all of the knobs. Except in the bathrooms, all of the hardware is copper plated and is developing a warm brown patina. ABOVE RIGHT A Chinese export porcelain bird and a Frances Palmer vase grace a table in the front hall. OPPOSITE Katie found this late nineteenth-century stained-mahogany sofa with its vivid ikat fabric at Christie's. The sconces are twentieth-century Swedish. OVERLEAF Portieres in swamp water–green linen, trimmed with tape and pink wooden beads, frame the opening from the stair hall to the living room.

LIVING ROOM

Knowing that she wanted to use pinks, reds, and greens in the living room, Katie was thrilled to find a muted antique Oushak carpet in an estate sale at Sotheby's in her desired color palette. The rug, the first item Katie and Peter bought for the house, had once belonged to San Francisco style arbiter Dodie Rosekrans, a contributing editor at *House & Garden* when Katie worked there. From there, the room took shape. Katie chose a pink tea paper, a wall covering that has a subtle texture both from the parchment and from the way the pieces overlap. To soften the space, Peter suggested adding portieres to the openings to the entrance and stair halls. Katie chose a muted green fabric for the portieres, curtains, and the pelmet that fills the arch over the large north-facing window, so the saturation of color—the watermelon pink of one sofa, the purple of the chairs, the blue of a second sofa—wouldn't be too overwhelming. Though Katie concedes she "went crazy with colors," their various values are skillfully balanced. The comfortable chairs and sofas are arranged around a marble mantel from Chesney's—a Soane design. With its lofty scale and delicate Federal-inspired details and antiques, the living room is a somewhat formal—almost grand—space, but Katie's exuberant color choices make it feel youthful and vigorous.

ABOVE Katie designed this lampshade in an Indian linen print for a pair of *famille noire* vases that she bought at auction and had converted into lamps. OPPOSITE The watermelon velvet covering the simple lines of the Lawson-style sofa adds a note of bold color at the north end of the living room. In contrast, Katie upholstered the club chair in various Pierre Frey fabrics, using coordinating prints for the border along the edges of the skirt and seat and on the arms—a technique she had admired at the Musée des Arts Décoratifs in Paris. Teddy approves. OVERLEAF The color scheme of the room plays off the ochre and red tones of the antique Oushak. Katie picks up the pinks of the tea paper in the furniture and in the embroidered pelmet.

OPPOSITE Peter found this 1929 painting of Stockholm at auction. Katie upholstered her grandmother's settee in a hand-blocked print with a grosgrain tape. The elephant garden seats are left over from Katie's store. The embroidered blue pillow is from Svenskt Tenn, a favorite shop in Stockholm. ABOVE Chesney's made the mantel after a design in the archives of Sir John Soane's Museum in London. Collages by artist Scott Hatt sit next to 1925 busts of Peter's father and his twin sister. OVERLEAF LEFT Katie needlepointed this pillow after an example she saw in a picture of a Jeffrey Bilhuber project. She blew up the image, counted the stitches, and chose her own colors. OVERLEAF RIGHT A painting of a beetle by Alfred Bierstadt, medallions of the architect Karl Friedrich Schinkel and the sculptor Augustus Saint-Gaudens, and a polished rock from Montana sit on the mantel.

ABOVE A mid-nineteenth-century sculpture of a woman representing the spirit of America is set on an inverted column capital, just as Peter found it at auction. OPPOSITE French doors, identical to the set in the entrance hall, lead to the east-facing porch.

Dining Room

One of two curved spaces in the house, the dining room is separated from the living room by a large vault flanked by two curiosity cabinets. Peter and Katie use the room every day and opted to leave it completely open to the kitchen. A round table—which has leaves that expand it to seat twelve—sits within the almost circular space, with the curve of the east wall window bay mirrored by an identical curve in the west wall. The curves in plan, which encompass the Duncan Phyfe–inspired reeded chair rail, play off of the curves in elevation, including the arched alcoves above the curiosity cabinets.

Katie wanted the dining room to coordinate with the living room and yet be very different. To accomplish this feat, she pulled in some yellow—in the curtains, the curiosity cabinets, and sconce shades—and tinged the rich mulberry color of the walls with pink to harmonize with the tea paper in the living room. The beveled glass of Magiscope, a sculpture by Mexican artist Feliciano Béjar, refracts the light streaming in from the porch, increasing the optical interest of the space.

ABOVE A green-glazed Buddhist lion is mounted as a lamp. OPPOSITE A broad, vaulted opening leads from the living room to the dining room. The windows beyond face south, overlooking the flower garden. To the left, bay windows face the porch and to the right, an open arch leads to the kitchen. Both the eastern and western walls are bowed out, giving the dining room its curved shape. A blue glass Louis Philippe chandelier hangs at center above the Regency-style mahogany dining table. OVERLEAF LEFT Curiosity cabinets flank the vault between the living room and the dining room. A nineteenth-century enamel pigment set, a gazing ball, and a watchmaker's lathe are displayed among architect's drafting tools. OVERLEAF RIGHT The texture of a vase by Frances Palmer contrasts with the crisp profile of Austrian crystal candlesticks.

ABOVE Flowers from Katie's cutting garden, including dahlias and garden roses, decorate the table. OPPOSITE The dining room is open to the kitchen; portieres of printed linen are drawn for dinner parties. The walls are lacquered in mulberry. Peter and Katie found the Regency-style gilt black lacquer chairs with cane backs and seats at auction.

KITCHEN

ALWAYS BRIGHT, THE KITCHEN ENJOYS DIRECT LIGHT FROM THE SOUTH AND WEST AND SHARED LIGHT from the dining room and front hall. One of the broad tripartite windows overlooks Katie's garden, bringing its colors into the room. There is a frieze of green wallpaper, a pinkish Moroccan tile backsplash, and an aubergine enameled stove, but all of the architecture—cabinetry, trim, and paneling—is carried out in a soft, warm off-white. In a cost-saving move, Peter and Katie opted for factory-made cabinets, which are integrated into the paneling and tied together by a common crown molding. And what might not be readily apparent but is something of a small revelation: each elevation—with the exception of the south wall—is perfectly symmetrical.

Peter and Katie didn't want the kitchen island to be the family gathering place. Rather, they saw the dining room as an extension of the kitchen and wanted to be able to move easily between the two. The island is given over to cooking—one of Peter's favorite pastimes—and he designed an étagère in the center with frosted glass shelves to store pots and pans. He'd seen versions of this in professional kitchens—particularly when he worked on the design for the Mark Hotel—but he added electrical outlets and built-in LED lights to turn the étagère into a source of warm light, especially welcome during dinner parties, when the ceiling lights would be too bright. Space against the south wall allows for a small table and chairs—perfect for morning coffee—and a desk, where Katie stores her garden notebooks.

ABOVE Katie keeps her smaller vases and her seed records in this pine desk in the kitchen. OPPOSITE The glass door beyond the desk leads to the mudroom and the garden. OVERLEAF Peter laid out the kitchen so that the cooking area is on one side of the island and the breakfast area is on the other.

OPPOSITE Dahlias from the cutting garden are displayed on the counter. Fragments of aquatic decorations from the original Coney Island aquarium are mounted on the wall above. ABOVE A stainless-steel-and-glass étagère atop the island provides convenient shelving for cookware. The cabinetry is capped with a crown molding that defines the lower edge of a wallpaper frieze.

BAR, POWDER ROOM,
AND MUDROOM

EACH OF THESE SMALL SPACES IS ARCHITECTURALLY RESOLVED. THE BAR IS HANDILY LOCATED BETWEEN the hall and the kitchen and can be closed off by a door. Located in the same position across the entrance hall, the powder room features Katie's wallpaper Turtle Bay, a design that was new at the time the house was built. One of her favorite patterns in the line, Katie thought it an appropriate tribute to the many turtles in their pond. Peter cleverly fitted out a whimsical mirror with a pair of elephant-form sconces found separately at auction. The mudroom, which opens out onto Katie's garden, is a catchall for boots, coats, and garden equipment. Its purple tile floor—laid here in horizontal strips—echoes the tone of the front hall floor.

ABOVE In the bar, glass shelves set on copper rails support a collection of colored-glass vessels. The counter is vertical-grain old-growth pine. OPPOSITE A small vestibule between the entrance hall and the study leads to the powder room and a coat closet.

ABOVE AND OPPOSITE The powder room features Katie's Turtle Bay wallpaper. Peter fitted the mirror, which was found at auction, with elephant-form sconces, and Katie designed grosgrain-trimmed shades. OVERLEAF LEFT Teddy pauses at the door to the mudroom, where Katie covered the floor with small, brick-shaped purple Moroccan mosaic tiles to fit the scale of the room. OVERLEAF RIGHT A collection of occupational tintype photographs flanks the mahogany coatrack.

STUDY

THE STUDY IS THE ONLY ROOM ON THE GROUND FLOOR THAT CAN BE FULLY CLOSED OFF. LIKE THE bedrooms, it has an extra layer of acoustical insulation in its walls and a concealed, drop-down, spring-loaded gasket that seals the bottom of the door. To give the study a cozy atmosphere—it's a room used most often in the evening—Katie painted the walls a deep shade of purple and chose a colorful Jobs Handtryck fabric with a dark background for the curtains. As a result, this room feels more inwardly focused—the perfect spot for curling up on the sofa with a book or for watching television. Bookcases framing the window display sculpture and bas-reliefs, wooden boxes, and other artifacts, including a miniature bronze of the Statue of Liberty that was sold to raise funds for the construction of the actual Statue of Liberty. Peter's interest in American history is reflected in the various pieces displayed on the walls and cabinets: a sketch of George Washington by Benjamin West, an *Anti-Slavery Constitutional Amendment Picture* by Powell & Co., a Declaration of Independence rendered as an illuminated manuscript by Arthur Szyk in 1950, tintypes of Union soldiers, and a letter from Theodore Roosevelt to Peter's grandfather.

OPPOSITE Katie upholstered the chair in a wool tartan and edged the fern-green sofa with caterpillar trim. The linen curtains are from Jobs Handtryck, a Swedish textile designer that is one of Katie's favorites, and the pair of brass lamps flanking the sofa are a typical Scandinavian model from the 1960s. ABOVE Katie designed this bell-shaped lampshade in linen with grosgrain trim. Like every lampshade in the house, it was made by Sue Wellott of Shades from the Midnight Sun. OVERLEAF LEFT An ambrotype portrait of a militia officer wearing a plumed shako hat, center, and *There Is Rest in Heaven*, an 1801 Washington mourning engraving, lower left, are among Peter's collection of American prints and photographs. OVERLEAF RIGHT As the only dark room in house, the study is a perfect retreat for reading or watching a movie.

FAME discovering to AMERICA.
The Heroes who first founded her Independance.

STAIR HALL

THE STAIR HALL SITS ON THE CROSS AXIS OF THE HOUSE, OPENING INTO THE FRONT HALL THROUGH A small vestibule and into the living room through a broader opening. Its landing occupies the semicircular bay that projects from the north side of the house, offering panoramic views of the pond to the west and the lake to the east. Here, the alignment of the two axes and their sightlines is most pronounced: in the stair hall, views of the land and of other rooms, both upstairs and downstairs, are dramatic and dynamic.

Katie lined the stair hall in Scraffito, a wallpaper she designed expressly for the space. Sgraffito was an ancient method of decorating façades: a layer of stucco was scraped away in patterns to reveal a contrasting color beneath. Here, the pattern of stone blocks of diamante rustication was inspired by the Schwarzenberg Palace in Prague. Katie printed the paper in a vivid French blue, evoking the color of old

---

ABOVE A 1920s portrait of a terrier named Snow hangs above an étagère on which rest a celestial globe and drafting sets from Peter's collection. OPPOSITE Katie's Scraffito wallpaper lines the stair hall. The door beneath the landing leads to the north hedgerow. The purple woolen stair runner is bound in red tape, and nineteenth-century Japanese lacquerware trays adorn the west wall.

The sgraffito walls of the Schwarzenberg Palace in Prague were the inspiration for Katie's Scrafitto wallpaper.

architectural blueprints. Against this backdrop, she added colors from the surrounding rooms—purple for the runner and red for its trim and for the shades of the serpentine sconces. The architectural aspect of the stair hall is thoroughly exacting, all of its elements echoing the curved shape of the space. Even the geometric stair railing incorporates a curved baluster in a nod to the arc of the balustrade on the second floor. The newel post—almost Danish or North German in spirit—seems solidly columnar but from above, it curls inward like a thin piece of paper. And everywhere that the architecture creates a pocket of space, that space is used. For instance, the back side of the curve accommodates a laundry chute.

ABOVE The newel post of the stair looks solid from the side but the top view reveals that it is a hollow, shell-like form. OPPOSITE Second-floor plan. OVERLEAF LEFT From the stair hall, the view extends along the north–south axis through the front hall, kitchen, mudroom, and out to the garden. Peter designed a cabinet to display antlers and serve as a base for a Victorian bird vitrine. OVERLEAF RIGHT The bombé windows at the second-floor landing look north. A Victorian convex mirror reflects the curved wall.

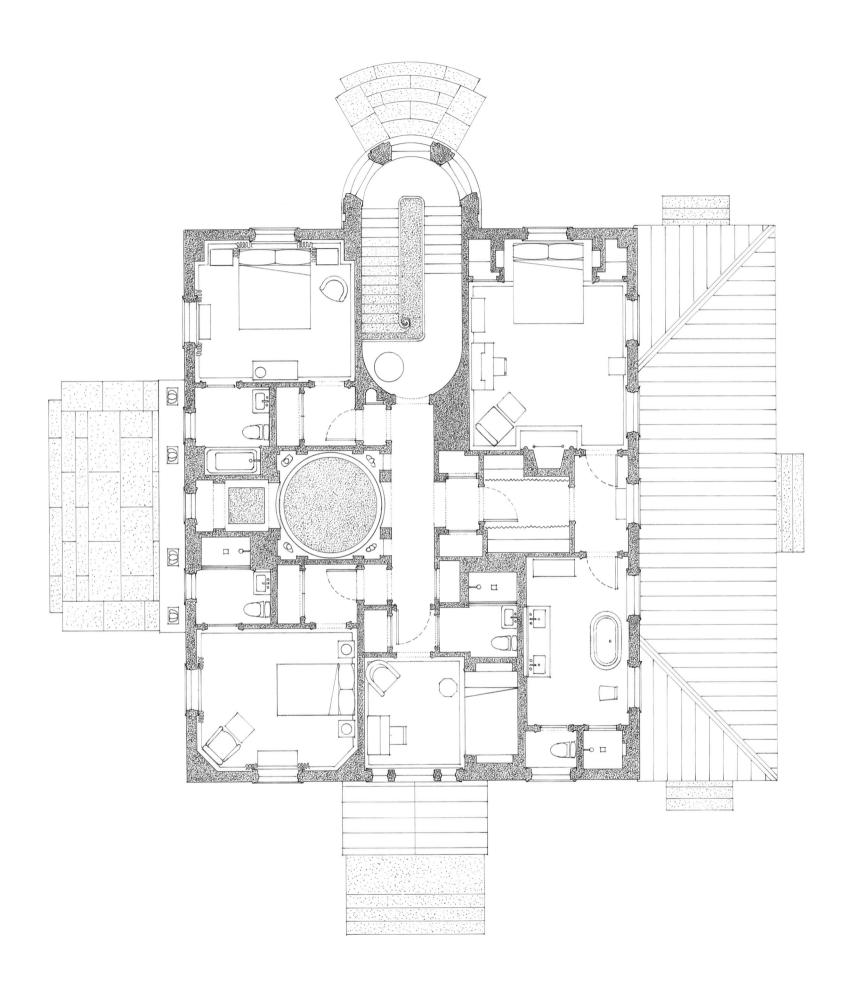

SECOND-FLOOR PLAN

BEDROOMS

KATIE AND PETER DECIDED TO KEEP THE BEDROOMS FAIRLY SMALL, BUT EACH ONE HAS ITS OWN BATHroom and each is entered through a vestibule with closets, as an extra measure of privacy. "It is nice to have closets that don't open into the room," Peter says, and, by locating closets outside the bedrooms, Peter and Katie could maximize wall space and let the rooms be self-contained. Large drainpipes on each corner of the house created a knock-out in one corner of each bedroom, but this anomaly was deftly absorbed into the plan and served to add design variation: in one room, for example, the walls are squared off in the corners; in another, they are angled.

At the end of the second-floor hall, on axis with the stair, is the first of three children's bedrooms: a cozy, square, blue-and-white space with a large three-part window and a bed set in an alcove. Around the time they began working on the house, Katie, Peter, and Gregory visited Potsdam—just outside Berlin— and toured the villas of Karl Friedrich Schinkel, the great nineteenth-century neoclassical architect working in Germany. Katie was smitten by a bedroom at Charlottenhof, a tented room carried out completely in blue-and-white stripes, from the walls and beds to the seats, with a subtle, interlacing red trim at the baseboard and ceiling. For her younger daughter, Gigi, she created her own variation, using a similar fabric for the walls and bed, a striking red trim around the moldings, and a playful set of Leontine linens in the same color palette. Swedish antiques and accent fabrics in bright primary colors give this distinctive room a fresh Nordic flavor.

Light brown wallpaper mimicking the look of pecky cypress creates a warm background for Katie and Peter's older daughter, Jane's, bedroom. This space—often a favorite of guests—is comfortable and inviting; its centerpiece is a luxurious bed. With the bed placed in front of the window, the curtains and valance provide the feeling of bed hangings. Katie was attracted to the Cowtan & Tout floral fabric for the curtains because it incorporated all of the reds, blues, purples, and greens she had used throughout the house and its cornucopia of appealing flowers are well defined and nicely drawn—something that was important to her. Meanwhile, for her son, Tony, Katie basically listened to her client. He asked for a dark bedroom, and his favorite colors are red and blue, so she used the same wood-grain-patterned wallpaper as in Jane's room but in a dark blue. A plush red bed, cozy rug, curtains in a coordinating ikat, and gold accents complete the picture.

OPPOSITE Inspired by the bed alcoves at Thomas Jefferson's Monticello, Peter set daughter Gigi's bed in a niche. Katie covered the walls and the ceiling of the niche in a striped linen trimmed with red grosgrain ribbon, an homage to a tented bedroom at Charlottenhof Palace in Potsdam. OVERLEAF LEFT The gilt rays of a sunburst-framed mirror catch the southern light. OVERLEAF RIGHT Katie upholstered the sweetheart-back chair in a Swedish linen print. The painting above the desk, *Forms of Trees and Clouds*, is by Karl Schrag, a twentieth-century modernist painter.

ABOVE Marbleized paper lines the back of the shelves in the niche. The brass lamp is from Svenskt Tenn and sports pleated shades in a Josef Frank fabric. OPPOSITE In keeping with the Swedish theme of Gigi's room, Peter found this nineteenth-century chiffonier with drop-down writing desk at Bukowskis, a Scandinavian auction house.

ABOVE Katie gave daughter Jane's room a wood-paneled effect using this pecky cypress–patterned wallpaper. The mahogany dresser has unusual overscale mercury-glass knobs. OPPOSITE Katie framed the north-facing window with curtains and a pelmet in a colorful English floral-patterned linen lined in plum. The bed features a headboard covered in a Fortuny fabric, a green velvet base, and a quilted Indian textile coverlet.

PRECEDING PAGES, LEFT Katie and Peter's son, Tony, wanted a dark room, so Katie used an inky blue version of the same pecky cypress–patterned wallpaper as in Jane's bedroom. The photographs on the far wall are by Christopher Makos from the 1980s. PRECEDING PAGES, RIGHT A detail of the curtain fabric, Ikat Splendide by Tissus Tartares. Its palette determined the color scheme of the walls and headboard. OPPOSITE Each bedroom has a distinct shape. Tony's room has angled corners. The club chair is upholstered in saffron mohair. The contact sheet is from a Cecil Beaton photo session with Twiggy in the 1960s. ABOVE Geometric-patterned concrete tile adds style to this small bathroom. The shower walls are clad in wood grain–patterned porcelain tile—a recent favorite of Peter's when budget is a main consideration.

MASTER SUITE

THE ENTRY VESTIBULE OF THE MASTER SUITE DOUBLES AS A DRESSING HALL. THE CLOSETS ARE CONCEALED behind curtains in Peony, a fabric from Katie's line, which make the space feel a bit like a tent. Beyond, a small, sunlit hall connects the bedroom to the north and the bathroom to the south. This approach gives the master bedroom a little bit of ceremony and a surprising amount of privacy for a small house. The color scheme—an array of greens, pinks, reds, and yellows—derives from a stunning pair of antique embroidered valances that Katie found at Cora Ginsburg's booth at the Winter Antiques Show in New York. Inspired by the green valances, Katie found a striking Donegal carpet with a green ground at Christie's and a vibrant green japanned Queen Anne–style bureau from Doyle, now the repository for Katie's seed envelopes. Although she admits to rarely using yellow in her designs, Katie employed a lot of it here—mostly in the form of a vivid, seemingly textured wallpaper—to draw out the intricate embroidery in the valances. As an example of trial by error, Katie decided to move the bed from the west wall into the window niche, preferring how the red headboard looked against its pink walls and curtains rather than against the yellow wallpaper. Following suit, Peter designed and installed built-in cabinets on either side, each with a reading light and charger. For the generously sized master bath overlooking the garden, Katie continued in the same palette, painting the wall a deeper shade of yellow and adding red and blue accents.

OPPOSITE The dressing hall is lined with curtains in Katie's Peony linen. The bench is a copy of a piece that Peter and Katie found in the flea market in Paris in 1994. Katie needlepointed a copy of the antique tapestry seat, following the original stitch by stitch. ABOVE In the master bedroom, a bouquet of 'Jane Cowl' dahlias sits below a study for a tapestry by Arthur Bowen Davies that was commissioned in Paris in the early years of the twentieth century.

The bed is set into a niche and flanked by recessed walnut nightstands that Peter designed. Katie's color scheme for the bed and the niche is a study in reds and pinks that refers to the brilliant colors in the turn-of-the-twentieth-century Donegal carpet. The photographs are from a 1936 portfolio of French châteaux by Jean Vincent that Peter bought in Paris when he was a student.

OPPOSITE Katie was drawn to the scale, presence, and color of the Queen Anne–style japanned secretary. The yellow wallpaper is a foil for the reds and greens in the carpet. The seat of the chair at the desk is covered in a fabric that Katie bought in the bazaar in Istanbul in the early 1990s. ABOVE Katie knew that she wanted a comfortable reading chair and ottoman next to a fireplace in the master bedroom. The Odom-style chair and ottoman are upholstered in a folk-inspired cotton print. The bolection is one of Peter's favorite mantel designs. Traditional Cut Stone carved this version. Elihu Vedder drew the charcoal study of feet above the mantel during his years in Paris.

ABOVE Katie bought a pair of late eighteenth-century southern European floral-embroidered green silk taffeta valances from Cora Ginsburg seven years before the house was built. To make sure they could both be used, Peter incorporated two windows into the design of the room. OPPOSITE An English mahogany whatnot from Cove Landing stands between the windows. The curtains are green silk with yellow silk banding.

OPPOSITE In the master bath, a freestanding tub set on the oak floor lends a country feel. The bamboo chair is a reproduction of an antique Chinese model. ABOVE A simple marble double washstand and a generous bank of deep, mirrored medicine cabinets are attractive yet practical. The orange rug is a tribal example from Morocco.

THE TRIBUNE

RATHER THAN A HOUSE WITH DISTINCT LEVELS AND TWO-DIMENSIONAL FLOOR PLANS, IN THIS HOUSE THE rooms are a series of interlocking volumes that address one another. This notion culminates in the tribune: most of the rooms refer to this space, including the entrance to the master suite, which lies directly on axis, and the front hall below. Top-lit halls and light wells were among Soane's favorite effects; he often used them in his work to heighten the experience of the space and, in his words, "keep the imagination awake." The parapet surrounding the round opening to the hall below has two segments pierced with a curved fish-scale pattern—constructed by Hyde Park Mouldings using a CAD model developed by Peter's office—while the large, square laylight, enhanced by a circular pattern of stars within a Greek key border—stickers that Peter put up himself—brings in light from above. Pilasters, set off against a green background, emphasize the circle-in-a-square effect and frame roundels by Abigail Tulis of the Judgment of Paris and Dionysus on the walls and four nineteenth-century busts, including likenesses of William K. Vanderbilt by Luella Varney and Daniel Macnee by George Edwin Ewing, on the corner shelves. As the space compresses toward the west, the vibrancy of the view out to the pond and woodland garden—seen through one of the house's three octagonal windows—becomes even more intense.

ABOVE Busts of William K. Vanderbilt and an unidentified nineteenth-century gentleman survey the tribune. The roundel, depicting the Judgment of Paris, was sculpted by Abigail Tulis. OPPOSITE A view toward the stair hall shows how the light from the tribune laylight spills into the second-floor hall.

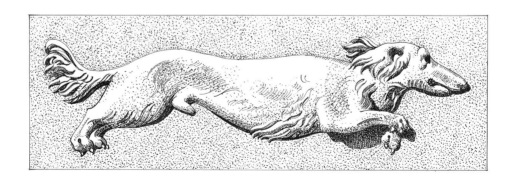

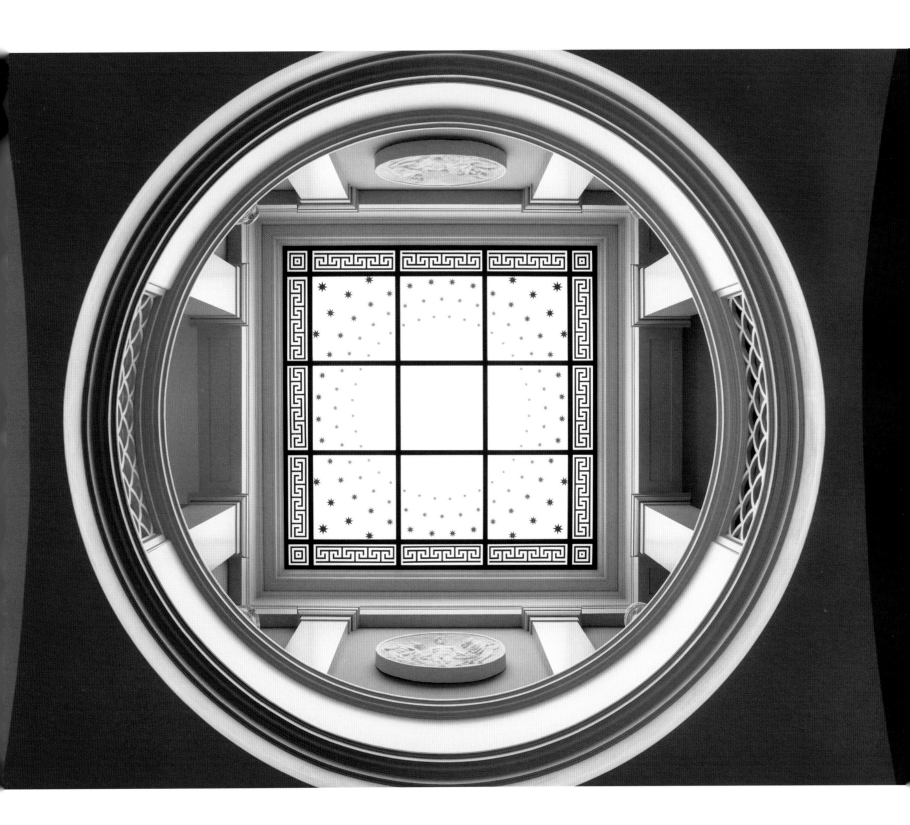

OPPOSITE TOP An east–west section of the center of the house shows how the laylight caps the tribune. OPPOSITE BOTTOM Sketch of the bas-relief dachshund on the frieze that ornaments the north façade of the house. ABOVE The stars and Greek key border decorating the laylight were laser-cut from custom-colored film and hand-pasted on each pane of glass by Peter.

OPPOSITE A curved fish-scale grille allows light to spill through from the center of the house. ABOVE The octagonal window frames a view of the pond and meadow beyond.

GARDEN

"MY FIRST GARDEN, ALMOST TWENTY-FIVE YEARS AGO, WAS A PREPACKAGED SEED GARDEN, complete with a plan, from the White Flower Farm. The directions told me everything I needed to know. I dug up a hard patch of clay soil to the required depth for proper drainage, planted my seeds, and—voilà!—it worked. I was so proud of it that I even showed it to my friend the garden designer Madison Cox, who was working down the road on my in-laws' garden on the water at Mishaum Point, Massachusetts. Thinking about it now, I cringe because it had the most gaudy color range imaginable, but it grew, and I was convinced that I did indeed have a green thumb. Since moving from New York City to Bronxville some twenty years ago, I've had many gardens (all in the same spot). I would dig up the beds completely every year, move plants around, try plants that required too much sun or too much shade, or were simply too tender for the locale. I learned a lot along the way, but always in the setting of an existing house and landscape. At Millbrook, however, I was confronted with a blank slate—an intimidating prospect for me as a self-taught weekend gardener. As the house was going up, I thought about the garden constantly, to the point of obsession. I started gathering information and inspiration from as many different places and people as possible."

Katie pored over books by Christopher Lloyd, the late owner and steward of Great Dixter in East Sussex, England; Ken Druse, whose works are "bibles for serious gardeners"; and Page Dickey, a friend who's written many books on her own garden as well as articles for *Gardens Illustrated* and blogs, including Matt Mattus's Growing with Plants and Margaret Roach's A Way to Garden. She went to lectures by Roach, Dickey, Marco Polo Stufano, Dan Hinkley, and Ed Bowen. She visited as many private gardens as she could and immersed herself in Wave Hill and the New York Botanical Garden in the Bronx and Stonecrop Gardens in Cold Spring, New York. When she learned of a plant or flower from a lecture or a book, she'd search for it in nurseries online and quite often take an impromptu trip to find it at Wave Hill to see how it was placed and how it looked in situ. After dozens of these visits, she claims to know Wave Hill, a perennial favorite, "like the back of my hand." Katie committed the layout and types of plantings to memory, even down to the number of plants and dimensions of each bed, eventually joining the garden's Friends of Horticulture committee. To keep track of her research, she filled three-ring binders with notes, pages of text, and photographs.

PRECEDING PAGES A view of the flower garden in summer looking south from the mudroom steps. ABOVE Moss grows between the reclaimed bricks that define the floor area beneath the pergola. OPPOSITE A ten-foot-tall hornbeam hedge creates an even, deep green backdrop for the garden, seen here in early spring displaying a lush mix of perennials, annuals, rare plants, shrubs, and bulbs.

The landscape architect Ed Hollander, who frequently collaborates with Peter's firm, designed the landscape plan for the entire property, including the hedgerows and trees. Katie gave Ed a list of trees she liked, old-fashioned varieties that Hollander likened to "grandma" trees, but Katie gravitated toward the idea of having a landscape of associations. She wasn't afraid to borrow ideas; she loved, for example, how the trees and plantings in one area of Stonecrop Gardens were reflected in a nearby pond and strove for a similar effect with newly planted birch trees on the northeast side of the pond in Millbrook. Inspired by the fragrance of Page Dickey's garden, she added the same Miss Kim lilacs to hers. To celebrate a recent birthday, Katie, Peter, and their daughter Jane went to England and toured the gardens at Great Dixter, Sissinghurst, RHS Garden Wisley, and Chelsea Physic Garden. These visits reinforced her sense that a garden of high visual impact, both in color and in texture, was the right approach for Millbrook. Adding to the challenge was the fact that her garden is located in USDA Plant Hardiness Zone 4B, a much colder environment than Katie expected. Other than help with general cleaning and weeding and quarterly visits by Timothy Tilghman, head gardener of Untermyer Gardens Conservancy in Yonkers, New York, all of the hard work rests on Katie's shoulders. Yet she is most happy when working in her garden and feels lucky indeed to engage in such a labor of love.

ABOVE A detail of one of the beds in spring. OPPOSITE The view from daughter Gigi's bedroom shows the garden's connection to the fields beyond.

FLOWER GARDEN

THE FLOWER GARDEN IS A ROOMLIKE SPACE ENCLOSED BY A DEER FENCE WITHIN A TEN-FOOT-TALL HORN-beam hedge that stretches around the perimeter, creating a backdrop of an even, deep green for Katie's extremely varied plantings—a lush mix of perennials, annuals, rare plants, shrubs, and bulbs. A critical, if unglamorous, part of Ed Hollander's design was robust infrastructure: the entire garden area was excavated prior to planting and a system of drainage and irrigation pipes was set in layers of gravel below newly imported topsoil that proved to be very fertile.

The greenhouse, a basic gardeners' model with a polycarbonate roof, constructed from a kit, stands against the garage wall and anchors the west end of the garden. This 10-by-16-foot structure is critical to the life cycle of the garden, particularly the annuals. In the early spring, after her seeds germinate in her basement in Bronxville with the aid of heating mats and lights, Katie transports them to Millbrook and places the trays of seedlings in the greenhouse on stone counters supported by aluminum piping—a detail copied from Wave Hill. A misting system, heater, and exhaust and circulation fans support a good growing environment. Since 20 percent of her garden is made up of annuals, the greenhouse allows Katie to get a head start on the season and to ensure that the plants will flower during the summer months. It also shelters her succulents, geraniums, tender potted plants, and summer bulbs in the winter.

Having gathered information and sources from many different places and people, Katie knew she wanted something along the lines of an English cottage garden—dense, overscaled, with a lot of color and contrasting texture. Though several friends encouraged her—unsuccessfully—to curb her instinct for variety and abundance, she decided that in her garden, "bigger would be better" and "less is a bore." Ed Hollander suggested that she keep it simple and limit herself to forty different types of plants. But with just one chance to use a friend's wholesale account at Sunny Border Nurseries, Katie enthusiastically ordered sixty-five. For some specimens, she ordered all of the cultivars, as she'd never grown them before and didn't know their habits. After initially laying out the beds, she asked Dennis Gendron of Twin Brooks Gardens—a local Millbrook nursery—to have a look. He warned her that she had about 40 percent more plant material than needed and showed her how to properly space the plants by removing some of the excess in one of the beds. But she wanted to use everything she'd ordered to achieve a lush and full effect quickly, so she put all 1,100 plants in the ground with the help of Dennis's crew.

OPPOSITE Just outside the greenhouse door is a *Malus sargentii* 'Tina', a bonsai-like flowering dwarf crabapple tree. TOP AND ABOVE In the greenhouse, Katie grows *Ricinus communis*, the castor oil plant (top), and *Nicotiana alata* 'Lime Green' (above), a long-blooming species of tobacco, from seed.

At Wave Hill, Katie was particularly drawn to the lighthearted exuberance of the flower garden and its vivid mix of plantings. Her garden is also exuberant, unfolding throughout the seasons as a series of vibrant groupings that create a riot of color and texture. A collector's garden, it includes a lot of everything—annual poppies and *Dianthus*, bachelor buttons, larkspur, sweet alyssum, flowering *Nicotiana*, *Verbena bonariensis*, *Salvia*, zinnias, *Tithonia*, dahlias, and sunflowers, many of which have self-seeded. But the groupings of these annuals, as well as shrubs, reoccur throughout the garden, tying it together and giving it a weighted presence that counteracts the annuals' wild flowering.

Crisp-edged bluestone paths divide the garden into fourteen beds, but the symmetry and formality of the plan blur as plants billow outward and upward in a rich tapestry of greens, blues, purples, pinks, reds, yellows, oranges, and whites. A path also runs from the mudroom, down the steps, and through the beds to a gate that opens to the farmland beyond.

At the center of the garden is a pergola—or outdoor dining room. Peter designed the pergola as a minimalist structure, opting for steel tubing with the least obtrusive profile possible so that Katie's vibrant plantings would have more impact. Soft-edged paving brick defines the floor area of the space while thin steel rods create a ladder for the 'New Dawn' roses, clematis, sweet pea, morning glory, and white wisteria, which will eventually drape the entire pergola, eliminating the need for the protective bamboo now in place. Around it, swaths of repeating perennials mingle with special plants—or specimens—that Katie has popped in.

Now that several years have passed, Katie has learned a lot by trial and error. She has edited out many plants that didn't contribute as much as she had expected or hoped and composted them all. "At least I'm not afraid of composting," Katie says with a laugh, "since it will all end up back in my garden." She is constantly pulling out plants, moving them around, and seeing what thrives. Because the garden isn't big enough to waste space on anything mediocre, any plant that doesn't have winning foliage, long flower time, or is simply not hearty enough goes. Some of her editing is driven by her refusal to use pesticides. She avoids lilies because of the red lily beetle population in Millbrook and late-season roses because they attract Japanese beetles. In coming years, she intends to introduce more grasses—she admires the linear grace and movement they add to English gardens.

An enchanted and fragrant oasis, the flower garden is an extension of the house—an outdoor room—that is easily accessible from the kitchen. Because the garden is visible through the wide windows of the house, the colors permeate the rooms that overlook it, creating a dynamic interplay between indoors and out that changes dramatically with the time of day and with the seasons.

ABOVE A collection of succulents and plants in the greenhouse includes some given to Katie by her friends Page Dickey and Bosco Schell. OPPOSITE Trays of seedlings line the stone counters of the greenhouse. Pots of tender plants have wintered over and are ready to be placed in the garden again.

Dahlia 'Penhill Dark Monarch'

Symphytum × uplandicum 'Axminster Gold'

Rabdosia longituba

Artemisia ludoviciana 'Valerie Finnis' and *Anemone* 'September Charm'

Nicotiana alata 'Perfume Deep Purple'

Tithonia rotundifolia 'Torch'

Tulipa 'Prinses Irene'

Baptisia 'Purple Smoke'

Kirengeshoma palmata

Allium aflatunense 'Purple Sensation'

Echinacea purpurea 'Virgin'

Iris germanica 'Abiqua Falls'

Tithonia rotundifolia 'Torch' and *Amaranthus* 'Hopi Red Dye'

Papaver somniferum 'Lauren's Grape'

Heuchera 'Frosted Violet'

Dahlia 'Karma Choc'

Centaurea montana

Paeonia lactiflora 'Karl Rosenfield'

Malus sargentii 'Tina'

Dahlia 'Gerrie Hoek'

Rosa 'New Dawn'

Tulipa 'Blue Spectacle' and 'Prinses Irene'

Allium giganteum

Viburnum plicatum 'Kerns Pink'

Pulmonaria and *Lamium*

Alchemilla mollis

Solanum pyracanthum and
Cordyline australis 'Atropurpurea'

Sedum 'Matrona'

Iris germanica 'World Premiere'

Iris sibirica 'Butter and Sugar'

Cuphea

Iris germanica 'Black Knight'

PRECEDING PAGES In the early summer, the bright pink of *Echinacea purpurea* 'Pica Bella', deep purple of *Papaver somniferum* 'Lauren's Grape', and the columnar fastigiate beech add color amid the many shades of green. OPPOSITE In the mid-spring, *Allium stipitatum* 'Mount Everest' rises above the low plantings, including *Amsonia* 'Blue Ice' with its lavender star-shaped flowers. THIS PAGE Spring flowers, clockwise from top left: *Baptisia* 'Carolina Moonlight', *Amaranthus* 'Hopi Red Dye', *Penstemon* 'Dark Towers', *Lilium* 'Chocolate Canary', *Artemisia ludoviciana* 'Valerie Finnis' and *Salvia verticillata* 'Endless Love', *Alchemilla mollis* behind *Lamium maculatum* 'Purple Dragon', *Hakonechloa macra* 'All Gold' and *Allium sphaerocephalon*, *Iris germanica* 'Lovely Senorita'.

OPPOSITE In late spring, the deep violet of 'Blue Spectacle' and the bright orange of 'Prinses Irene' tulips ignite the bed next to the mudroom door with color. ABOVE In the same bed, the *Hydrangea paniculata* 'Limelight' comes into bloom after the tulips have faded. OVERLEAF Katie and Peter gathered branches from a shadbush to make trellises for climbing clematis. Purple, burgundy, and pink flowers, including *Geranium macrorrhizum* 'Bevan's Variety' and *Aquilegia vulgaris var. stellata* 'Black Barlow', dominate the garden in spring.

OPPOSITE The velvety leaves of lamb's ears (*Stachys byzantina* 'Countess Helen Von Stein') and the feathery leaves of *Calamagrostis × acutiflora* 'Karl Foerster' against the deep burgundy of *Amaranthus* 'Hopi Red Dye' create a wide of range of textures. TOP Looking southwest toward the pergola. ABOVE The bearded iris (*Iris germanica* 'World Premiere') with its deep purple and white flowers thrives in early spring.

TOP AND ABOVE In the late summer, the table in the pergola is set for dinner, adorned with Katie's loose arrangements of purple and blue clematis and delphinium. OPPOSITE Peter designed the pergola as a minimalist structure, using steel tubing with an unobtrusive profile to allow the plantings to predominate. Stainless-steel rods create a ladder for the climbing 'New Dawn' roses, clematis, sweet pea, morning glory, and white wisteria that will eventually cover the entire pergola.

OPPOSITE Katie collected *Amaranthus* 'Hopi Red Dye' seeds from her friend the ceramicist Frances Palmer's garden two years ago. They have now self-seeded throughout the garden. ABOVE The thick, velvety foliage of the lamb's ears expands out over the edges of the garden path. Its dense, low-growing form anchors the *Penstemon* 'Dark Towers' that billow upward.

ABOVE The deep purple spikes and starry florettes of the *Eucomis comosa* 'Sparkling Burgundy' grow among the *Amsonia*. OPPOSITE *Echinacea purpurea* 'Virgin', *Cotinus coggygria* 'Golden Spirit', and the black-leafed *Dahlia* 'David Howard' intermingle in one of the beds.

OPPOSITE The early morning sun hits the pergola and highlights the summer annual *Tithonia*. ABOVE 'Jane Cowl' dahlias decorate the al fresco breakfast table.

OPPOSITE By late summer, the beds are a multicolored mosaic of textures. ABOVE The late summer *Anemone tomentosa* 'Robustissima' in one of the garden's shady beds.

ABOVE LEFT Self-seeded Shirley poppies (*Papaver rhoeas*), larkspur (*Consolida regalis*), and *Amaranthus* run through the beds and beyond. ABOVE RIGHT *Viburnum plicatum* 'Kerns Pink' and *Heuchera* 'Obsidian'. OPPOSITE TOP Self-seeded 'Lauren's Grape' poppies in front of *Amsonia* and *Echinacea*. OPPOSITE BOTTOM *Salvia verticillata* 'Endless Love' and *Sedum* 'Frosty Morn'.

ABOVE *Allium sphaerocephalon* reach for the sun, spilling over the north path. OPPOSITE Potted succulents are grouped on the steps leading to the mudroom door.

OPPOSITE In the summer, the *Tithonia* reach their full height. ABOVE By the end of the summer, the spiky, vivid red seedpods of the castor oil bean proliferate. OVERLEAF *Heuchera* 'Marmalade' and *Cornus alternifolia* 'Golden Shadows' (Pagoda dogwood) create a lush autumn palette of greens, oranges, and burgundies.

ABOVE A shade bed in the southwest corner of the garden includes *Hosta*, *Hakonechloa macra*, painted fern (*Athyrium niponicum*), and *Viola*. OPPOSITE While Katie does some weeding in November, Teddy enjoys a bit of sun.

CUTTING GARDEN

ACROSS THE POND AND BEHIND THE EXISTING BARN LIES KATIE'S CUTTING GARDEN, SET AGAINST A BACK-drop of cornfields belonging to the neighboring farm. A rustic cedar gate and a deer fence enclose a series of long, rectangular raised beds where Katie grows dahlias—eighty different types—peonies, cosmos, zinnias, sunflowers, and other annuals. She also grows vegetables, herbs, and berries, including tomatoes, potatoes, carrots, leeks, beans, beets, lettuce, rhubarb, watermelon, blackberries, and raspberries. Throughout the summer and fall, Peter and Katie share an abundance of freshly cut flowers and just-picked vegetables with their friends.

OPPOSITE The cutting garden is located on the western edge of the property beyond a grove of birch trees. TOP Self-seeded nigella (*Nigella damascena*) has taken over one of the beds. ABOVE A plump watermelon is ready to be picked. OVERLEAF A deer fence with a rustic cedar gate encloses the raised beds that make up the cutting garden. A drip system for irrigation is in place, as Katie attends to the garden only on weekends. The cornfields of the neighboring farm mark the boundary of Peter and Katie's property.

TOP LEFT The 'Jane Cowl' dahlia is just one of the eighty different types of dahlias in the garden. TOP RIGHT Self-seeded cosmos (*Cosmos bipinnatus*) have sprouted all over the cutting garden. ABOVE The sunflower 'Velvet Queen' grows among dahlias, cosmos, and irises. OPPOSITE Bamboo stakes support Katie's many dahlias.

OPPOSITE Green Zebra tomatoes are one of several varieties of tomatoes in the cutting garden. TOP LEFT Black Krim, Brandywine, and Pruden's Purple tomatoes are ready to be picked. TOP RIGHT A bamboo trellis allows air to circulate around the tomatoes to prevent disease. ABOVE A self-seeded tomato plant and the castor oil plant (*Ricinus communis*) flourish in the compost heap. OVERLEAF LEFT The *Dahlia* 'Gitts Perfection' peaks in late summer. OVERLEAF RIGHT Cosmos, dahlias, and sunflowers in the late summer.

Woodland Garden

On the sloping swath of land west of the house, Katie is creating a woodland garden under the canopy of existing oaks and maples and new understory trees—red and white redbuds, dogwood, and magnolias—along an undulating path down to the pond. Peter suggested planting an abundance of ferns in this area, and although Katie also envisioned something simple and low-maintenance, she wanted some color and lots of texture and variation. At the suggestion of Timothy Tilghman, she introduced arcing beds under the trees for woodland perennials and herbaceous plants she has collected. To the beds she has added bulbs—daffodils, *Colchicum*, *Galanthus*, *Puschkinia*, *Scilla*, and *Eranthis*—and plants such as native ginger, woodland phlox, hellebores, variegated Solomon's seal, Virginia bluebells, *Trillium*, twinleaf, bloodroot, and *Epimedium*. Recently planted ostrich ferns at the back of each bed will eventually tie the garden together. At the end of the woodland shade path, a simple footbridge over the stream that feeds the pond from the south leads to a stone terrace centered on a fire pit. From here, Peter and Katie can take in the sweep of the property and imagine new projects in the years to come.

ABOVE *Muscari armeniacum* 'Valerie Finnis' were among the first bulbs planted in the woodland garden. OPPOSITE Katie introduced arcing beds under the woodland trees at the suggestion of Timothy Tilghman of Untermyer Gardens. Daffodils are in full bloom in early spring. OVERLEAF Under the existing oak and maples, Katie added red and white redbuds, dogwood, and magnolias. A simple footbridge spans the stream that feeds the pond from the south.

ABOVE Linden trees rim the west side of the parking court. OPPOSITE Peonies under crabapples on the north side of the house bloom in May.

ABOVE Mature trees line the dirt lane north of the house. OPPOSITE Looking over the pond toward the woodland garden. OVERLEAF In November, the Ostrich fern (*Matteuccia struthiopteris*) plugs that Katie planted in the spring have started to grow. Eventually the ferns will tie the garden together.

ABOVE An egret lingers under the weeping willow on the eastern edge of the pond. OPPOSITE Native grass thrives at the edges of the pond. OVERLEAF In fall, the hills to the north are ablaze with color. PAGES 222–23 The fire pit next to the pond has become one of Peter and Katie's favorite places on the property.

SOURCES

ARCHITECTURE

Peter Pennoyer Architects
PARTNERS-IN-CHARGE:
James Taylor, AIA, LEED AP,
and Peter Pennoyer, FAIA
DESIGN DIRECTOR:
Gregory Gilmartin
ASSOCIATES:
Matthew Cummings,
Arthur Rollin, Cecilia Rodgers,
LEED AP, Timothy P. Kelly,
John Gibbons, Daniel Berkman,
Philip Davis, Genevieve Irwin

ppapc.com

Structural Engineer
Albert Putnam, PE
Albert Putnam Associates, LLC
albertputnam.com

Mechanical Engineer
Andrew J. McPartland, PE,
  LEED AP
(207) 899-5533

Envelope Consultant
James R. Gainfort, AIA
(212) 736-3344

Civil Engineer
Wade Silkworth, PE
Silkwork Engineering

**Environmental Consultant/
Pond Design**
Roy T. Budnik, PhD
Roy T. Budnik & Associates, Inc.
(845) 485-6911

Lighting Design
Conceptual Lighting, LLC
conceptuallighting.com

Audio Visual
Ben Rosner
eHome
e-home.com

General Contractor
Westerley Construction LLC
Grant Stinchfield, President
Colin Calhoun, Project Manager
westerleyconstruction.com

**Excavation and Pond
*Étagère and Laylight**
Kyle Mooney
KJM Excavating, Landscaping,
  & Welding, Ltd.
(914) 474-7621

***Stair**
King & Company
kingstair.com

Windows and Doors
Architectural Components Inc.
architecturalcomponentsinc.com

***Columns**
Tidewater Millwork
tidewatermillwork.com

Radiant Heat
Warmboard Inc.
warmboard.com

Millwork
Terry Baldwin
Stanford Enterprises Inc.
stanfordenterprisesinc.com

Shutters
Southern Shutter Company
southernshutter.com

***Hardware**
Elliot Lowe
Lowe Hardware
lowe-hardware.com

Wood Flooring
Mountain Lumber Company
mountainlumber.com

Appliances
Viking Range, LLC
vikingrange.com

Plumbing Fixtures and Fittings
Waterworks
waterworks.com

***Plaster Moldings**
Hyde Park Mouldings
hyde-park.com

Bas-Relief Panels and Roundels
Abigail Tulis
abigailtulis.com

Living Room Mantel
Chesney's
chesneys.com

***Master Bedroom Mantel**
Traditional Cut Stone Ltd
traditionalcutstone.com

*Items designed by
  Peter Pennoyer Architects

INTERIOR

Katie Ridder Inc.
PARTNER:
Lizzie Bailey
PROJECT MANAGER:
Danielle Kelling
ASSOCIATES:
Anne Spilman
Olga Dykunets

katieridder.com

Accessories

Antique Textiles Galleries
antiquetextilesgalleries.com

Christopher Spitzmiller, Inc.
christopherspitzmiller.com

Frances Palmer Pottery
francespalmerpottery.com

La Forge Française
laforgefrancaise.com

The Old Print Shop
oldprintshop.com

Shades from the
  Midnight Sun
(914) 779-7237

Antiques

Alexander Cohane
alexandercohane.com

Cove Landing
(212) 288-7579

David Duncan
davidduncanantiques.com

Gerald Bland
geraldblandinc.com

Sutter Antiques
sutterantiques.com

Auction Houses

Bukowskis
bukowskis.com

Christie's
christies.com

Doyle New York
doylenewyork.com

Leslie Hindman Auctioneers
lesliehindman.com

Rago
ragoarts.com

Skinner Auctioneers & Appraisers
skinnerinc.com

Sotheby's
sothebys.com

Stair Auctioneers & Appraisers
stairgalleries.com

Swann Auction Galleries
swanngalleries.com

Carpets

Studio Four NYC
studiofournyc.com

Embroidery

Penn & Fletcher
pennandfletcher.com

Fabric and Wallpaper

Fortuny
fortuny.com

Harbinger
harbingerla.com

Holland & Sherry
hollandandsherry.com

Jobs Handtryck
jobshandtryck.se

John Stefanidis
johnstefanidis.com

Nobilis
nobilis-usa.com

Pierre Frey
pierrefrey.com

Svenskt Tenn
svenskttenn.se

Tissus d'Hélène
tissusdhelene.co.uk

Furniture

Anthony Lawrence Belfair
anthonylawrence.com

Charles H. Beckley, Inc.
chbeckley.com

Lighting

The Urban Electric Company
urbanelectricco.com

Visual Comfort & Co.
visualcomfort.com

Linens

Area Home
areahome.com

John Derian Company
johnderian.com

Leontine Linens
leontinelinens.com

Paint

C2 Paint
c2paint.com

Tile

Mosaic House
mosaichse.com

GARDEN

Garden Design
Katie Ridder

Landscape Architecture
Edmund Hollander
Stephen Eich
Hollander Design Landscape
   Architects
hollanderdesign.com

Garden Consultant
Timothy Tilghman
Untermyer Gardens Conservancy
untermyergardens.org

Garden Assistant
Amy Pelletier Clark

Bulbs

Brent and Becky's Bulbs
brentandbeckysbulbs.com

Endless Summer
endlesssummerflowerfarm.com

K Connell Dahlias
connells-dahlias.com

The Lily Nook
lilynook.mb.ca

Meadowburn Farm
meadowburnfarm.com

Old House Gardens Bulbs
oldhousegardens.com

Swan Island Dahlias
dahlias.com

Van Engelen Inc.
vanengelen.com

Plants by Mail

Annie's Annuals & Perennials
anniesannuals.com

Avante Gardens
avantegardens.com

Broken Arrow Nursery
brokenarrownursery.com

Camellia Forest Nursery
camforest.com

Digging Dog Nursery
diggingdog.com

Far Reaches Farm
farreachesfarm.com

Joy Creek Nursery
joycreek.com

Logee's
logees.com

Opus
opusplants.com

Peony's Envy
peonysenvy.com

Pine Knot Farms
pineknotfarms.com

Plant Delights Nursery, Inc.
plantdelights.com

Seeds

Great Dixter House & Gardens
greatdixter.co.uk

High Mowing Organic Seeds
highmowingseeds.com

Hudson Valley Seed Library
seedlibrary.org

Ivy Garth Seeds & Plants, Inc.
ivygarth.com

Johnny's Selected Seeds
johnnyseeds.com

Park Seed
parkseed.com

Sarah Raven
sarahraven.com

Select Seeds
selectseeds.com

Stonecrop Gardens
stonecrop.org

Turtle Tree Seed
turtletreeseed.org

Wild Garden Seed
wildgardenseed.com

Wisley
rhs.org.uk/gardens/wisley

Wood Prairie Farm
woodprairie.com

Trees and Perennials

Twin Brooks Gardens
twinbrooksgardens.com

The entrance on a stormy morning, before the snow plow arrived.

ACKNOWLEDGMENTS

WE HOPE THAT OUR BOOK CONVEYS THE COLLABORATIVE NATURE OF MAKING OUR HOUSE and gardens. So many people, most of whom we continue to work with on other projects, played important roles in the process. We have listed all of the significant participants in the Sources section of the book. Each should know that we are grateful and that inclusion in our book is our resounding endorsement.

We are especially fortunate to know Gregory Gilmartin, who has been our friend and colleague for more than thirty years. Gregory challenges us to do our best work at every turn, reminding us that excellence is our standard and inspiring us with his deep knowledge of architectural history and his brilliant designs. His role in this project reflects our decades of thinking about architecture together, and his designs are the backbone of the house.

Within Peter Pennoyer Architects, we thank my partner, Jim Taylor, who managed a project with a budget that was stretched at every turn and with a client who was at his side asking questions more frequently than any architect deserves. Cecilia Rodgers took the lead drawing the project, with assistance from Matthew Cummings, Arthur Rollin, Tim Kelly, John Gibbons, Daniel Berkman, Philip Davis, and Genevieve Irwin.

Within Katie Ridder Inc., we are very grateful to my partner Lizzie Bailey, project manager Danielle Kelling, Anne Spilman, and Olga Dykunets for their invaluable support, from scheming the interiors to sourcing and all of the myriad tasks involved when dealing with some 129 different vendors and sources.

We are grateful to Mish Tworkowski, who recommended Candy Anderson, a Millbrook Realtor, who patiently led us over hill and dale for weeks until we reached the place where we said, "This is it."

Our neighbors, welcoming us even before we were under construction, provided much-needed encouragement and valuable tips on local resources. This group included Kirk Henckels and Fernanda Kellogg; Mish Tworkowski and Joseph Singer, and Gerry and Mita Bland. We also thank Bill Bontecou, who lived in the barn apartment, took care of the land, and helped us understand the history and culture of the place.

We were fortunate to have Ed Hollander and his associate Stephen Eich as our landscape architects. They knew how to restore the land and weave in new features while respecting the sense of place. We thank Dennis Gendron of Twin Brooks Gardens, who provided trees and shrubs, planted the hedgerows, and built the cedar fences and the cutting garden's raised beds. We thank Page Dickey for her friendship and advice and for the plants she gave us from her own garden.

For the photography, which brings the house and garden to life, we thank Eric Piasecki, who brought his enthusiasm, imagination, and artistic eye to a challenging project.

For her research and for writing the essay, we are deeply grateful to our friend and long-time co-author Anne Walker. For her role in supporting the research, writing, photography, and general organization and air traffic control, we thank Lucinda B. May. For his exquisite renderings, we thank Anton Glikin. For elegantly balancing the photography, renderings, and text, we thank the book's designer, Celia Fuller.

Finally, we are proud to continue our relationship with Vendome Press. Our publisher, Mark Magowan, and editor, Jackie Decter, have our deepest gratitude. Their smarts, enthusiasm, and ambitions for this book gave us confidence and made the process a pleasure.

Peter Pennoyer and Katie Ridder

First published in the United States of America by
THE VENDOME PRESS
www.vendomepress.com

Copyright © 2016 Peter Pennoyer and Katie Ridder
Text copyright © 2016 Anne Walker
Introduction copyright © Peter Pennoyer
Photographs copyright © Eric Piasecki

ISBN 978-0-86565-329-0

EDITOR JACQUELINE DECTER

PRODUCTION DIRECTOR JIM SPIVEY

DESIGNER CELIA FULLER

ILLUSTRATOR OF PLANS, ELEVATIONS,
AND SECTIONS ANTON GLIKIN

Library of Congress Cataloging-in-Publication Data

Names: Pennoyer, Peter, author. | Ridder, Katie, author. | Piasecki, Eric.
Title: A house in the country / Peter Pennoyer and Katie Ridder with Anne
    Walker ; Photography by Eric Piasecki.
Description: New York : Vendome Press, 2016.
Identifiers: LCCN 2016020072 | ISBN 9780865653290 (hardback)
Subjects: LCSH: Pennoyer, Peter -- Homes and haunts -- New York
    (State) -- Millbrook. | Ridder, Katie--Homes and haunts -- New York
    (State) -- Millbrook. | Architect-designed houses--New York
    (State) -- Millbrook. | Country homes -- New York (State)--Millbrook. |
    Millbrook (N.Y.) -- Buildings, structures, etc. | BISAC: ARCHITECTURE /
    General. | ARCHITECTURE / Interior Design / General. |
    ARCHITECTURE / Landscape. | DESIGN / Interior Decorating. |
    ARCHITECTURE / Sustainability & Green Design.
Classification: LCC NA737.P393 A35 2016 | DDC 728.809747--dc23
LC record available at https://lccn.loc.gov/2016020072

This book was produced using acid-free paper, processed
chlorine free, and printed with soy-based inks.

PRINTED IN CHINA BY OGI

FIRST PRINTING

PHOTO CREDITS

All photos by Eric Piasecki, with the exception of the following:
Pages 19 left and 22 left: Peter Paige; Page 19 right: Municipal
Archives, Department of Records and Information Services, City
of New York; Page 20: Drawing by Gavin Macrae-Gibson, Robert
A. M. Stern Architects; Page 21: Drawing by Peter Pennoyer; Pages
22 right and 25 bottom: Reto Halme; Pages 26–27: Scott Frances;
Page 28: Fernando Bengoechea; Pages 32, 43 top, and 44 bottom:
Jonathan Wallen; Page 33: Rendering by Irina Shumitskaya; Page
36: Sidney S. Benham; Page 37: John Foreman's Big-Old Houses.
com; Page 42: Maine Forms of American Architecture; photo
by Richard Cheek; Page 43 bottom: Drawing by Anton Glikin;
Page 44 top: © By Courtesy of the Trustees of Sir John Soane's
Museum; Page 45: 3D rendering by Timothy P. Kelly; Page 120 top:
© Vincenthanna | Dreamstime.com

PAGE 1 A deer-form coat hook
in son Tony's bedroom hall.

PAGES 2–3 Katie, Peter, and
Teddy enjoying the fall foliage.

PAGES 4–5 Bird's-eye view of
the flower garden, facing east.

Pages 6–7 View of the tribune
from the front hall below.

PAGES 8–9 The east side of the
house on a snowy afternoon.

PAGE 10 The living
room fireplace is lined in
herringbone-patterned brick.

PAGES 12–13 Detail of the
Queen Anne–style japanned
secretary in the master bedroom.